EASY TO MAKE
PUPPETS

EASY TO MAKE

PUPPETS

Joy Gammon

ANAYA PUBLISHERS LTD LONDON

First published in Great Britain in 1993
by Anaya Publishers Ltd, Strode House,
44–50 Osnaburgh Street, London NW1 3ND

Editor Patsy North
Design by Design 23
Photographer Steve Tanner
Illustrator Terry Evans

British Library Cataloguing in Publication Data

Gammon, Joy
Easy to Make Puppets. –
(Easy to Make Series)
I. Title   II. Series
745.592

ISBN 1 85470 042 1

Typeset by Servis Filmsetting Ltd, Manchester, UK
Colour reproduction by Scantrans Pte Ltd, Singapore
Printed and bound in China.
Produced by Mandarin Offset

CONTENTS

Introduction

Puppet-making is a craft that anyone can enjoy. This book introduces a wonderful collection of puppets, some simple, some elaborate, but all easy to make.

Puppets have been around since the days of the cave-dwellers, and they have always been used for the same purpose; they help us to tell stories. The first puppets were probably shadows. Imagine sitting in your cave on a freezing night, with the dark threatening to overwhelm the fire as the storyteller throws shadow pictures of monsters and men on to the stone walls. Later, puppets were used in combination with actors to tell stories; certainly Punch has been a costumed man as well as a puppet in his time. Now we can look back on a long tradition of beautiful puppet-making and theatre in all parts of the world. Think how many stories, plays and ballets are based on puppets, as well as the actual puppet plays themselves.

Puppets can be made from all kinds of things, and if you try out the ones in this book you will use everything from knitting wool to papier mâché, from fabric to clay, even your socks. All over the world people make use of wood, paper, fabric and any other material that will help to create a fascinating variety of puppets. They come to life as you animate them, and you will know that you are making progress with your puppet-making when you begin to talk to your characters as you put them together. It is possible to become surprisingly involved with puppets. I met a puppeteer recently whose Mr Punch was Best Man at his wedding.

Puppets in action
You can use your puppets to tell stories, to play games or to put on a full-scale play, and they can help you in all sorts of ways. They can act out situations which

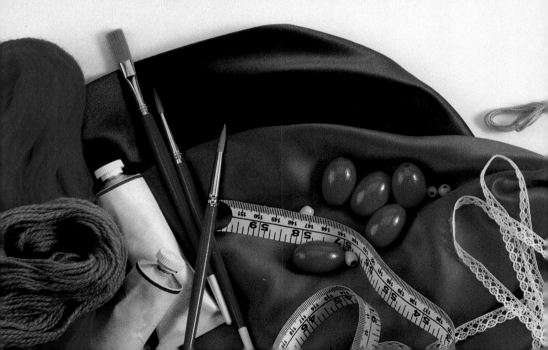

we might have difficulty in acting out ourselves, and they can say things which we would like to say, but find hard to express. It is much easier to portray the spectacular, the fantastic or the fabulous in puppet theatre than it is on the ordinary stage. Even animals are much more credible as puppets than they are as costumes on people. A puppet circus, for example, works much better than a stage full of actors dressed up as elephants, lions and horses.

This book is a beginning. My intention is to start you off on ways of creating puppets which I hope you will then elaborate upon and adapt in any way you like to create the characters from your imagination.

That's the way to do it . . .

Safety notes

All the techniques used in this book are the ordinary craft methods which are familiar to most people, but however much craft work you have done before, do remember always to work as safely as you can.

If you use craft knives, always do so with great care, working away from you on a surface well padded with newspaper. Store craft knives with their blades covered and keep them out of reach of small children.

Always use non-toxic glues, taking care to work in a well-ventilated room and to replace caps and lids on glues after use.

You may make some of your puppets for very small children to use or to play with. Make sure that you use soft materials like fabric, wool and paper for these puppets, and that they are decorated with embroidery or firmly sewn-on pieces rather than beads, buttons or stuck-on decoration that could be eaten. Any sharp material like metal or splintery wood should not be used for younger children.

Materials and techniques

In the instructions, the specific materials that you will need to make each particular puppet are listed, but not the ordinary things needed for any craft work like glue, scissors, needles and thread. If any unusual tools are required, they will be listed.

The straight seams and longer lines of stitching used in assembling the puppets have been stitched on a sewing machine, and this certainly saves time. But if you prefer, all the sewing for the puppets can easily be done by hand.

ONE

Finger and hand puppets

❧

Paper bag tiger

Puppets made from paper bags, like this beautiful tiger, are probably the simplest of all, and are ideal for young children to make for themselves.

Materials

10 × 5in (25 × 12.5cm) yellow flat-bottomed paper bag
Scraps of white, yellow, brown, black and pink paper

Making the tiger

1 Trace the templates where necessary and cut out from coloured paper varied black stripes, yellow ears, white ear linings and beard, brown eyes, black pupils, and a pink nose. Stick these firmly on to the paper bag.

2 Draw in details with a black pen, and add a white dot to each eye.

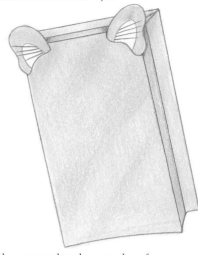

Stick on the ears so that they stand up from the head.

The faces on paper bag puppets can be drawn with felt-tipped pens or chalks, painted or created with stuck-on shapes. Hair can be made from wool, strips of cut paper or lampshade fringing. Puppets can have necklaces, crowns and hair ornaments made from paper, sequins, doilies or paper stars. The list of possible characters is endless: family and friends, animals, pets, characters from stories, caricatures, goodies, baddies, monsters, to name but a few. Older children could make a diver using a polythene bag with a face showing through from the inside, or an astronaut from a bag sprayed with silver metallic paint, with the face peering through a cellophane window. (Remember, though, never to use any polythene bags for puppets for small children.) Because these puppets are so simple, they can be adapted very freely in the spirit of the simple cartoon.

trace off actual size

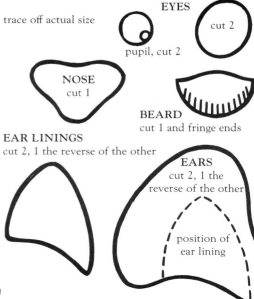

EYES
cut 2

pupil, cut 2

NOSE
cut 1

BEARD
cut 1 and fringe ends

EAR LININGS
cut 2, 1 the reverse of the other

EARS
cut 2, 1 the reverse of the other

position of ear lining

Octopus

The basis of this easy-to-make puppet is simply a glove and a pompon. It can even be worn when out and about, but be careful, they often go about in twos . . .

Materials
Stiff card sufficient to cut two 4in (10cm)
    pompon circles
Part ball of green knitting yarn
Green glove, preferably rubber
Pair of bought toy safety eyes, or felt or
    card circles

Preparation
1 Trace the pompon circle and cut 2 out of stiff card.

2 Make a pompon about 3½in (9cm) in diameter as shown on page 103 of the Better Techniques section. Do not make the pompon too dense, as it needs to be soft for the next stage.

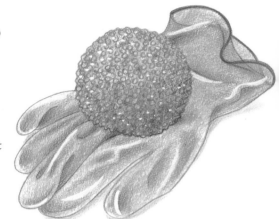

Flatten one side of the pompon and glue centrally to the glove.

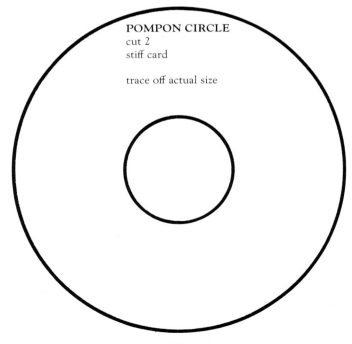

POMPON CIRCLE
cut 2
stiff card

trace off actual size

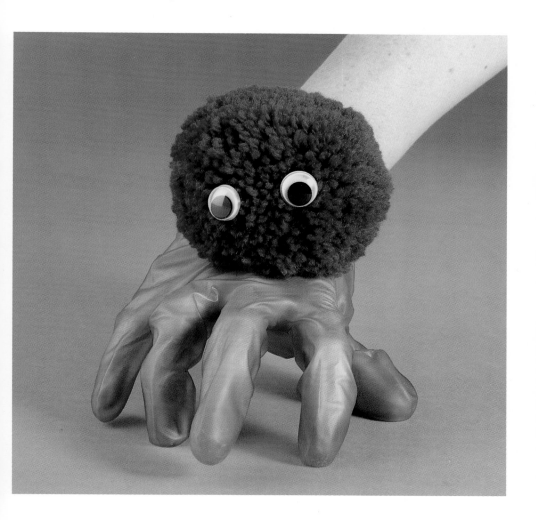

Making the octopus

3 Flatten one side of the pompon so that it becomes a dome shape and glue it to the centre back of the glove. If the glove is fabric or knitted, the pompon could be sewn on.

4 Cut circles of white and black felt and stick together to make goggle eyes, or use bought eyes if you wish. Stick on the eyes towards the knuckle side of the pompon.

Creepy creatures

These puppets make wonderful creepy creatures. Anything with lots of legs will work well – black spiders, red crabs or monsters of any and every colour. They can be real functioning gloves too, and you could add feelers, claws, scales or any decoration. In a puppet show they are very versatile because they are hands and so can express themselves, pick things up and carry them, and relate to other puppets, shaking hands, poking puppets in the ribs and so on.

Felt finger puppets

These little puppets representing fairy-tale characters are so easy to make, and yet they can be quite elaborate. Decorating them with colourful scraps is very satisfying.

Materials

Small pieces of felt in the main colours plus contrast scraps of felt including beige or flesh colour

Scraps of fabric, lace, stiff net, cords, ribbons and yarn

Beads, glitter powder and sequins

Scraps of straw and stick

Making the basic puppet

1 Trace the pattern for the body shape. For each puppet, cut 2 body shapes in the main colour and sew them together, leaving only the bottom edge open. The wizard is red, the elf green, the fairy pink and the witch black.

2 For each puppet, cut a ¾in (2cm) diameter circle of beige or flesh-coloured felt for the face. Embroider blue or black eyes with French knots and a small red mouth in back stitch. Stick the face on the front of the puppet, near the top.

HAT CROWN
cut 1
felt
wizard, elf and witch

trace off actual size

HAT BRIM
cut 1
felt
witch only

BODY SHAPE
cut 2
felt

FAIRY'S WINGS
cut 1
stiff net

14

Wizard

3 Cut out a beard shape and fringes of hair in white felt. Trace the pattern for the crown shape only of the hat and cut out in red felt. Sew it into a cone and sew the white hair fringes around it. Sew this fringed hat on to the top of the head and the beard to the bottom of the face. Trim the hair if necessary, so that the face can be seen. Knot a cord around the Wizard's middle and secure it with a stitch at each side. Sew or stick on multicoloured sequin stars.

Elf

4 Trace the pattern for the crown shape only of the hat and cut out in red felt. Sew it into a cone, then sew on to the top of the head. Fold to one side and catch down. Sew a bead on to the point of the hat. Sew red ribbon as a belt around the Elf's middle and embroider a yellow buckle on it. Embroider a cord around the neck and add a gold bead.

Fairy

5 Sew lace and ribbon scraps around the Fairy's middle to form a skirt. Sew strands of yellow knitting yarn to the top of the head as hair and secure into bunches. Sew a flower sequin at the centre front of the hair. Trace the pattern for the wings and cut out from stiff net. Run a line of glue all around the edge and sprinkle with glitter powder. Allow to dry and then sew into place on the back of the puppet.

Stick the embroidered face to the sewn-up body shape.

Because finger puppets are so small, you can get really carried away with the decoration because it will not take long or cost very much. A word of warning though. These puppets fit an adult finger or that of an older child. You may wish to make them smaller for a younger child, but remember that they are not suitable for very young children as they are small enough to be swallowed, like some of the bits with which they are decorated.

Finger puppets are ideal for groups of characters like extras at crowd scenes, as one puppeteer can instantly be ten characters which is a great help with casting problems. However, avoid having too many wide puppets like the Fairy with her wings, especially on one hand, as they will clash and tangle.

Sew strands of knitting yarn to the fairy's head for hair.

Witch

6 Trace the patterns for the crown and brim of the hat and cut out in black felt. Sew the crown into a cone, then sew the brim around the bottom edge of the crown. Sew lengths of black yarn around the inside of the hat brim at the back as hair, then sew the hat on to the top of the head. Gather a square of thin black fabric along one edge to form a cloak, hemming if necessary. Sew the gathered edge of the cloak around the neck and add a grey cord tie. Make a besom broom by tightly tying a small bunch of straw around a short stick. Sew the broom to the front of the witch.

Sew the witch's hat crown into a cone and sew on the brim.

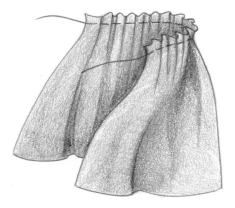

Gather the witch's cloak along the top edge of the black fabric

Whiskered walrus

This appealing walrus hand puppet has a lot of character with his long tusks and beady eyes. Felt is ideal to use as it is easy to sew and does not fray.

Materials
12 × 10in (30 × 25cm) piece of grey felt
Small pieces of pink and white felt
Black and white embroidery thread
2 small round black beads
Very small quantity of toy stuffing

Preparation
1 Draw a pattern on squared paper from the graph pattern below. Put in all marks and words. Cut out the pattern pieces. Cut out the top and bottom halves of the walrus in grey felt, and the top and bottom mouth parts in pink felt. Cut out 2 tusk shapes in white felt.

Making the walrus
2 Stitch together the top and bottom mouth parts along their straight edges only.

3 Taking care that all seams will appear on the same side of the completed work, and matching shapings, stitch together the top mouth part and the top of the walrus's body around the front curve of the mouth. In the same way stitch together the front curves of the bottom mouth part and the bottom of the walrus's body. Now join the 2 straight side seams, stitching the top and bottom of the walrus's body together. Turn right side out.

4 Stitch each tusk into a cone, stuff and attach by its open end to the underside of the top jaw, placing the 2 tusks symmetrically.

1 square = 1in (2.5cm)

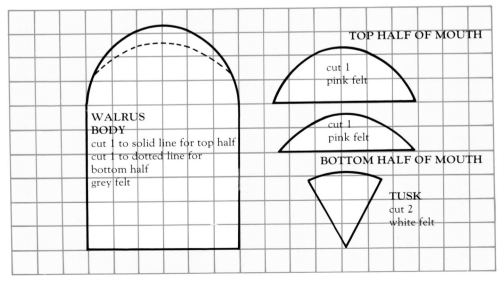

WALRUS
BODY
cut 1 to solid line for top half
cut 1 to dotted line for bottom half
grey felt

TOP HALF OF MOUTH
cut 1
pink felt

cut 1
pink felt

BOTTOM HALF OF MOUTH

TUSK
cut 2
white felt

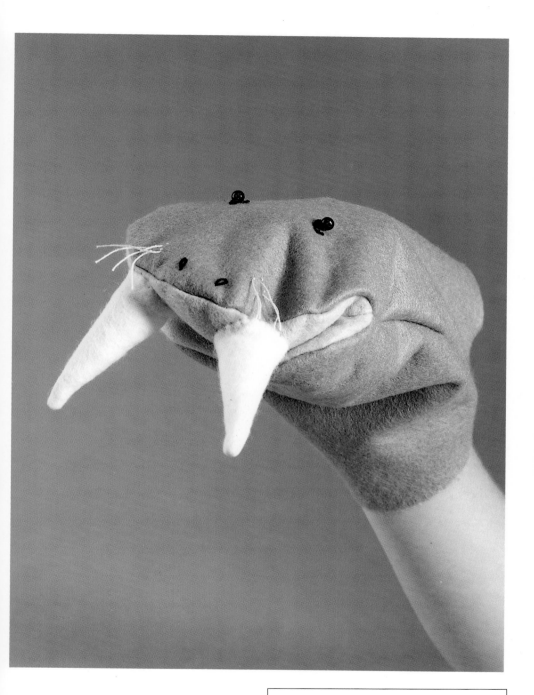

Finishing
5 Sew on the beads as eyes, and embroider a black eyelid line and black nostrils. Sew short whiskers of white thread in place.

Other creatures with this simple body shape could include seals and seal pups, snakes and caterpillars, whales, dolphins and sharks.

19

Dog sock puppets

Sock puppets are simple to make but are very expressive. These two mischievous dogs – a terrier and a spaniel – will be ready for action in next to no time.

Materials
(For each dog puppet)
1 plain sock in a doggy colour
Small pieces of felt in black, white and
   brown
Optional toy safety eyes and dog nose

Preparation
1 Try the sock on your hand to see if the heel looks logical as part of the dog, perhaps as the back of his head. If you want to remove the heel, turn the sock inside out and stitch a smooth curved line through both thicknesses of sock. This will straighten the heel bump when the sock is turned the right way out again. Avoid cutting the sock because it will probably fray.

Stitch a curved line to remove the heel.

Making the dog
2 If making a felt nose, trace the pattern and cut out in black felt. Stick it on to the sock. If you are using a bought dog nose, push the shank through the sock and secure with the washer.

3 If making felt eyes, cut 2 white circles about 1¼in (3cm) in diameter, then 2 slightly smaller brown circles, 2 black circles slightly smaller again and 2 very small white circles. Stick the circles one on top of the other to make the eyes. Stick each eye into position on the sock. Alternatively, attach bought safety eyes in the same way as for the nose.

4 Trace the pattern for the ears, using either the droopy spaniel shape or the triangular terrier shape. Cut out in felt. Sew on the droopy spaniel ears from underneath, with the ear across the top of the dog's head while you sew, so that when they droop back down they have a natural curve at the top. Make a pleat in the triangular terrier ears to give the characteristic shape. Sew to the head, catching each one down at the front.

Sock puppets are great for any character or animal that has a long nose. Dogs are ideal, and you could experiment with all sorts of breeds. Attach a pompon with a ribbon bow for a poodle's head, or cover a white sock with black spots for a dalmatian. If you have a very large sock, gather the fabric up into the blunt wrinkled nose of a bulldog. Other creatures which make especially good sock puppets are horses and donkeys with ribbon harness and wool manes; sheep, lambs and cows; snakes with sequin scales; rats and mice; pigs; dinosaurs and monsters. As well as using felt for features, try sequins, embroidery, ribbons, buttons, wool and paint.

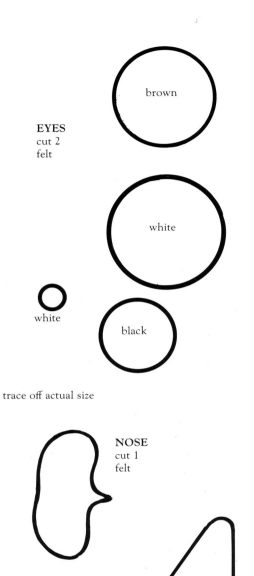

EYES
cut 2
felt

brown

white

white

black

trace off actual size

NOSE
cut 1
felt

TERRIER EARS
cut 2
1 black felt
1 white felt

Finishing

5 Tuck in the toe of the sock to form a mouth. Work a line of back stitch either side of your thumb position to secure the lower jaw.

Tuck in the toe of the sock to form a mouth and sew either side of the thumb position.

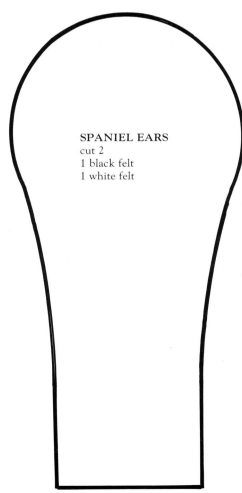

SPANIEL EARS
cut 2
1 black felt
1 white felt

Folded paper frog

This frog snapping at a fly is based on a child's folded paper puzzle.
It is important that the paper is an exact square and that
the folds are very straight and accurate.

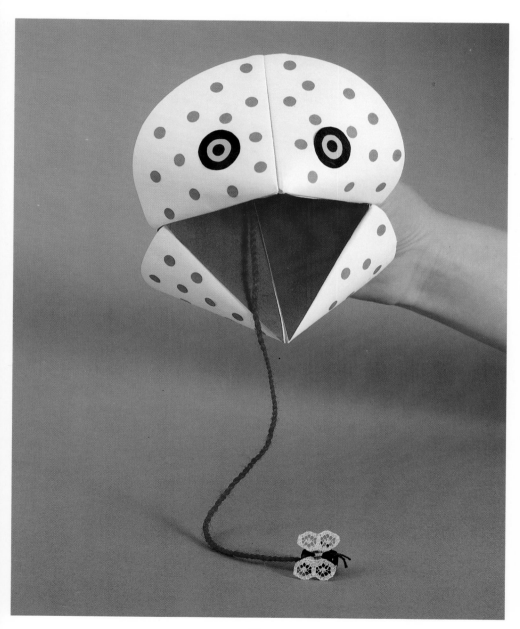

Materials

11in (28cm) square sheet of white paper
Two 2¾in (7cm) squares of red gummed
　　paper
Scraps of black and yellow gummed
　　paper
Green gummed paper spots
10in (25cm) length of red cord or thick
　　yarn
Two round black beads
Tiny scrap of white or cream lace
Scraps of fine black thread

Making the frog

1 Following the diagrams and pressing
each fold firmly to leave a line, fold the
paper as exactly as possible in the
following way:

2 First fold each corner into the exact
centre of the square.

3 Turn the folded square over.

4 Fold each of the corners into the exact
centre of the square.

5 Fold the resulting square in half one
way, then open this fold out again. Turn
the square through 90° and fold it in half
the other way, then open this fold out
again.

6 Open out all the folds and flatten the
paper. Draw a line rounding off each
corner. Cut these corners off.

7 Apply the decoration to the correct
areas of the folded pattern. Cut the two
red squares of gummed paper in half
diagonally and stick these four triangles
in the positions shown. Stick on two eyes
made from circles of yellow and black
gummed paper. Decorate the areas
indicated with green gummed paper
spots. Mark the sections which are to be
glued.

8 Refold the paper as before. With the
thumbs and index fingers of both hands
placed one under each curved corner of
the paper, push the points of the outer

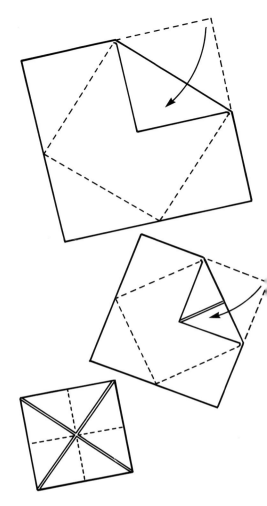

a = position of red gummed paper
● = position of eyes
b = areas to decorate with green gummed paper
　　spots
c = areas to be glued

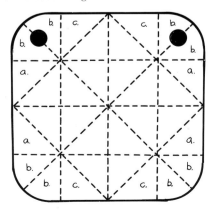

24

corners forward to create the frog. Find the areas which were marked to be glued and stick them together to form the top and bottom of the mouth, which then becomes completely red.

Fly

9 Stick the two beads together to form the body. Cut wing shapes from the lace and stick them to the centre of the back. Stick 3 fine black threads centrally to the underside of the fly to give 6 legs and stick on black thread antennae.

10 Stick one end of the red yarn to the centre back of the frog's mouth and the other end to the back of the fly.

These paper creatures can be any operable size and colour; the trick is extreme accuracy in the folding. The paper should not be too thick or it will not fold properly. For the same reason, it is difficult to make these puppets very small. The frog can be used as a kind of cup-and-ball game with the fly, and similar puppets could include any lizard-like creature with a gaping mouth, a dinosaur, a chameleon or possibly a bird. They could be eating anything you like, however disgusting.

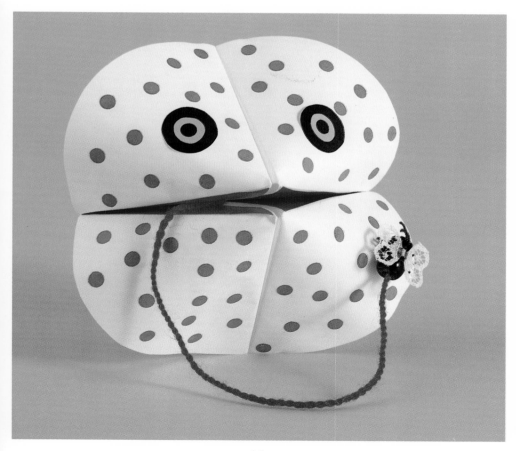

Nativity scene

This scene consists of nine puppets all made in the same basic way – Mary, Joseph, the Archangel Gabriel, the three Kings and the three shepherds. The Infant Jesus lies asleep in his crib.

Materials

For each of the 9 similar puppets

16½in (42cm) square piece of fine fabric for the skirt

6¼in (16cm) square piece of fine beige or flesh-coloured fabric for the head OR, if the skirt fabric is transparent, 16½in (42cm) square piece

Square, triangle or rectangle of fabric for the cloak of which one side is at least 11in (28cm)

Square of thin card or thick paper large enough to roll around the puppeteer's index finger to make a tube at least 2½in (6cm) long

Small quantity of stuffing

Selection of braid, trim, knitting and embroidery yarn, felt or beads

Additional 3¼in (8cm) square of thin card for characters with haloes (Mary, Joseph and Gabriel)

Additional 6 × 9½in (15 × 24cm) piece of card for Gabriel's wings

Optional glitter powder and metallic paint for crowns, haloes and wings

Short length of stiff ribbon or card for the crown of each king

For the Infant Jesus

Small square of white fabric such as a handkerchief

2½in (6cm) square of fine beige or flesh-coloured fabric

2½in (6cm) square of thin card for halo

Silver and gold glitter powder

Very small quantity of stuffing

For the manger

6¼ × 4in (16.5 × 10cm) sheet of card

Making the basic puppet

1 From the skirt fabric cut a circle 16½in (42cm) in diameter. Cut a circular hole 5¼in (13cm) in diameter in the exact centre of this piece.

2 *If the skirt fabric is opaque*, cut a circle 6¼in (16cm) in diameter from the beige fabric. With the right side of the beige fabric to the wrong side of the skirt fabric, pin the beige circle centrally to fill the hole in the middle of the skirt.

3 *If the skirt fabric is transparent*, cut a second circle 16½in (42cm) in diameter from the beige fabric. With the right side of the beige fabric to the wrong side of the skirt fabric, pin the two circles together so that their edges match.

Setting the scene

This Nativity can be used as a static scene, or the puppets can be moved about as puppets should. A simple backdrop of starred paper and straw on the floor would be sufficiently evocative, but you could add as many details as you like, perhaps additional animals or the gifts which the visitors brought.

Other scenes could be made in the same way; any story with a large cast of human characters would be suitable. These puppets are also simple enough for children to make, with lots of fun involved in the decoration and the trimming.

4 Hem the outer edges of the larger circle or circles if the fabric is likely to fray.

5 Run a gathering thread around the edge of the inner circle through both fabrics together, using small, neat stitches. Turn a small hem to the wrong side of the skirt fabric at the same time if required. Do not pull the gathering thread tight at this stage.

6 Roll the 2½in (6cm) long piece of card into a tube to fit the index finger of the puppeteer and secure with adhesive tape. Make a ball of stuffing which will comfortably pad the central circle of beige fabric when it is gathered. Stick to the top of the tube. Place the gathered fabric centrally over the stuffing and the tube. Pull the gathering thread tight enough to contain all the stuffing within the ball of fabric which is now the head, but not so tight that it squashes the tube. Fasten the gathering thread off firmly.

Features

7 Using black or brown embroidery thread, embroider very simple features. The eyes consist of four chain stitches in a simple downward curve. The small mouth is a line of straight stitches in red, pink or a neutral contrasting colour if the character requires it. Mary has very fine embroidered eyelashes.

8 On all the male characters except Gabriel, create a beard by sewing lengths of knitting yarn in suitable colours around the chin. Trim to different shapes and lengths to suit the characters.

Finishing

9 Experiment with the fabric for the cloak, either folding it or not, and placing it square on or as a triangle. Choose a different size and style for each figure. Decorate the cloak if required with braid, beads or ribbon, then catch it into position with a few invisible stitches. Add any other suitable decoration such as a scrap of sheepskin on a shepherd, 'jewels' on the Kings and stars on Mary.

10 Make small cylinders of stiff ribbon or thin card as crowns for the three Kings. Decorate with gold paint, jewels or glitter and catch down with a few stitches on to the top of their heads.

11 Cut 3 circles of card 3¼in (8cm) in diameter for the haloes of Mary, Joseph and Gabriel. Paint or spray these circles silver, put a line of glue around each one and add glitter powder. When dry, stick each halo to the back of the puppet's head.

12 Trace the pattern for Gabriel's wings and cut out from folded card. Paint or spray the wings silver. Using glue, mark feather shapes on the wings and add glitter powder. When dry, stick the wings into position at the centre back neck.

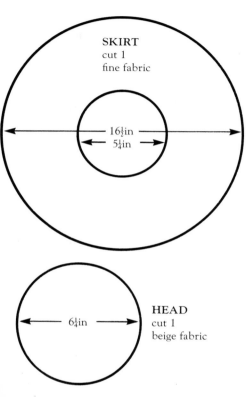

SKIRT
cut 1
fine fabric

16½in

5¼in

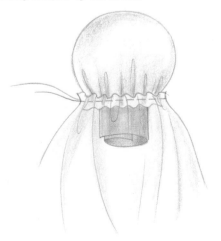

HEAD
cut 1
beige fabric

6¼in

Place the gathered head and skirt fabric over the stuffing and pull up the thread.

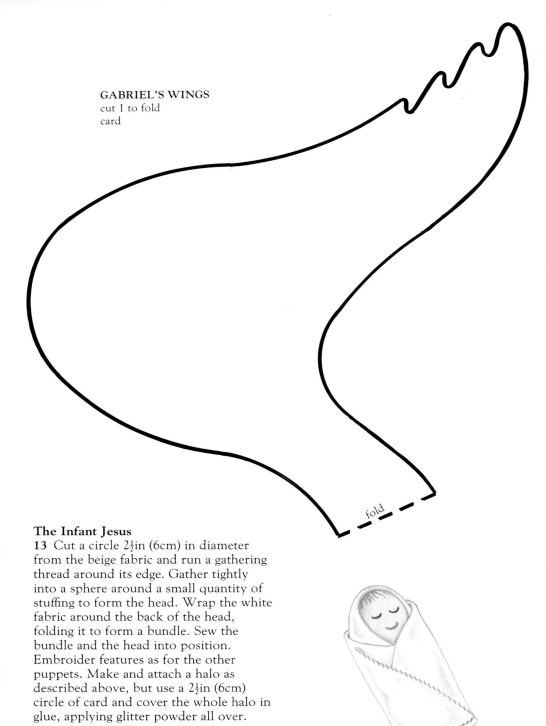

GABRIEL'S WINGS
cut 1 to fold
card

fold

The Infant Jesus

13 Cut a circle 2½in (6cm) in diameter from the beige fabric and run a gathering thread around its edge. Gather tightly into a sphere around a small quantity of stuffing to form the head. Wrap the white fabric around the back of the head, folding it to form a bundle. Sew the bundle and the head into position. Embroider features as for the other puppets. Make and attach a halo as described above, but use a 2½in (6cm) circle of card and cover the whole halo in glue, applying glitter powder all over.

14 Trace the manger shape on to card and cut out. Score along the fold lines, fold and stick down the tabs to assemble. Paint to look like wood.

Wrap white fabric around the head of the Infant Jesus and sew into position.

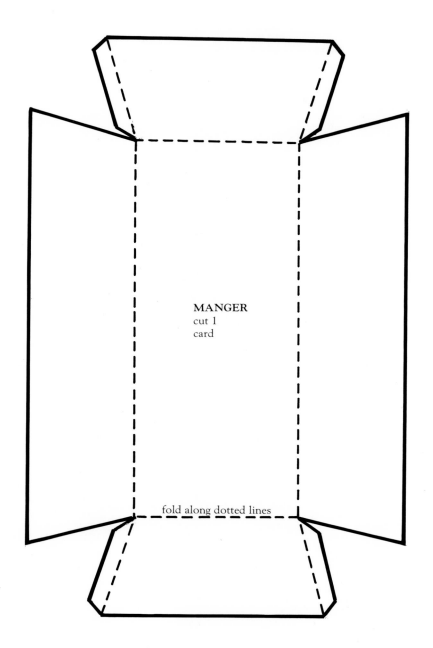

MANGER
cut 1
card

fold along dotted lines

TWO

Glove puppets

Hairy monster

This fearsome monster will bring shrieks of delight from his audience with his sharp claws, goggle eyes and green body covered in dangling hair.

Materials
12in (30cm) square piece of green felt
Lengths of assorted green and brown
  wools
Leaf-shaped sequins for claws
2 toy safety eyes

Preparation
1 Draw a pattern on squared paper from the graph pattern on page 36. Put in all marks and words. Cut out the pattern pieces.

2 Cut out 2 body pieces and 4 arms from the green felt.

Making the monster
3 Leaving the bottom edges and the marked arm positions unstitched, stitch together the 2 body pieces around their outer edges, matching the shaping.

4 Match the arm shapes into 2 pairs and stitch each pair together around the complete curved edges only. Stitch the arms into the openings in the side seams of the body so that they point upwards.

Finishing
5 Cut the wools into lengths of about 8¾in (22cm) and, knotting one' end of each length of wool, thread the other end through the felt from the inside using a large sewing needle. Pull the wool through until stopped by the knot. Repeat this at random all over the front of the monster's body until he is as hairy as you wish. Stitch longer strands of brown yarn on top of the head to give the effect of hair.

6 Attach the eyes and sew on the sequins as claws.

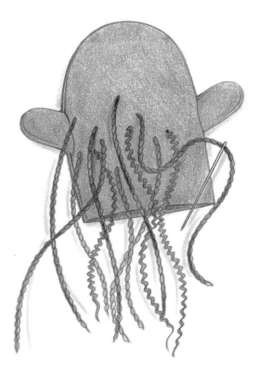

To make the hairy front, thread lengths of wool through from the back of the felt with a large sewing needle.

Sew leaf-shaped sequins to the monster's arms for sharp claws.

34

1 square = 1in (2.5cm)

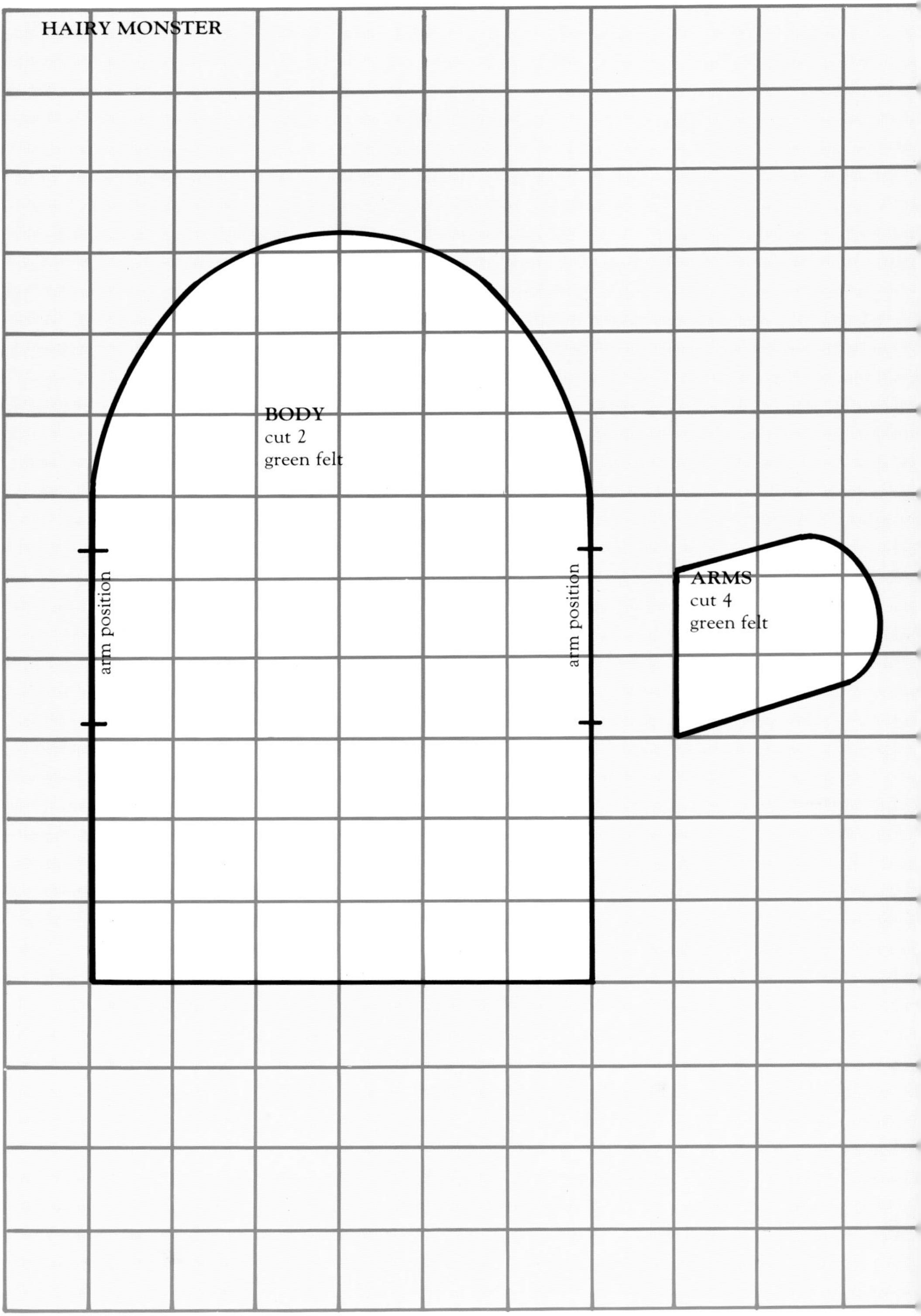

HAIRY MONSTER

BODY
cut 2
green felt

arm position

arm position

ARMS
cut 4
green felt

Sunflower

There is no reason why glove puppets have to be people or animals;
they can be vegetable too. This cheerful sunflower has an
opening behind each leaf for your thumb and little finger.

Materials

Two 9 × 5in (23 × 12.5cm) pieces of mid-green felt

One 6 × 2½in (15 × 6cm) piece each of light and dark green felt

8in (20cm) square of bright yellow felt

Green embroidery thread

6in (15cm) diameter lightweight paper or polystyrene dish, not more than 1½in (4cm) deep

3in (7.5cm) diameter circle of orange gummed paper

Scrap of black gummed paper

2 round black beads

Preparation

1 Draw a pattern on squared paper from the graph pattern on page 39. Put in all marks and words. Cut out the pattern pieces.

2 Cut out 2 body shapes in mid-green felt. Cut out 1 leaf in light green felt, 1 leaf in dark green felt and 12 petals in yellow felt.

Making the sunflower

3 Sew the 2 body pieces together around the outer edge, omitting the straight bottom edge and the two marked parts of the side edges, which will be the openings for the thumb and little finger of the puppeteer. Adjust these openings, if necessary, to suit the puppeteer. Choose whether the puppet is to be right- or left-handed and be careful to keep the puppet the right way round as you attach the details because it now has a definite front, with the little finger opening higher than that for the thumb.

4 Arrange the leaves on the front of the puppet so that they cover the openings at either side of the body, thus hiding the thumb and finger of the puppeteer. Using embroidery thread in a different green, catch down each leaf to the body with a central rib of back stitch, continuing this rib to the top of the leaf.

5 Stick the orange gummed paper circle into the bottom of the dish. Cut out a black gummed paper mouth and stick on to the orange circle. Stick on black beads for the eyes.

6 Arrange the petals evenly around the edge of the dish and stick them by their points to the outer edge of the orange circle. Lightly stick down the petal centres to the top rim of the dish.

7 Firmly stick the head to the top front of the body.

Field of flowers

If you have enough puppeteers it would be fun to make a whole field of sunflowers, two per operator, remembering to reverse the finger and thumb holes on one puppet of each pair so that it can be used on the other hand. Any flower with a corolla of petals could be made in this way, and they could, of course, be in any colour.

The sunflower's leaves hide the finger and thumb openings.

Sticking on the petals.

square = 1in (2.5cm)

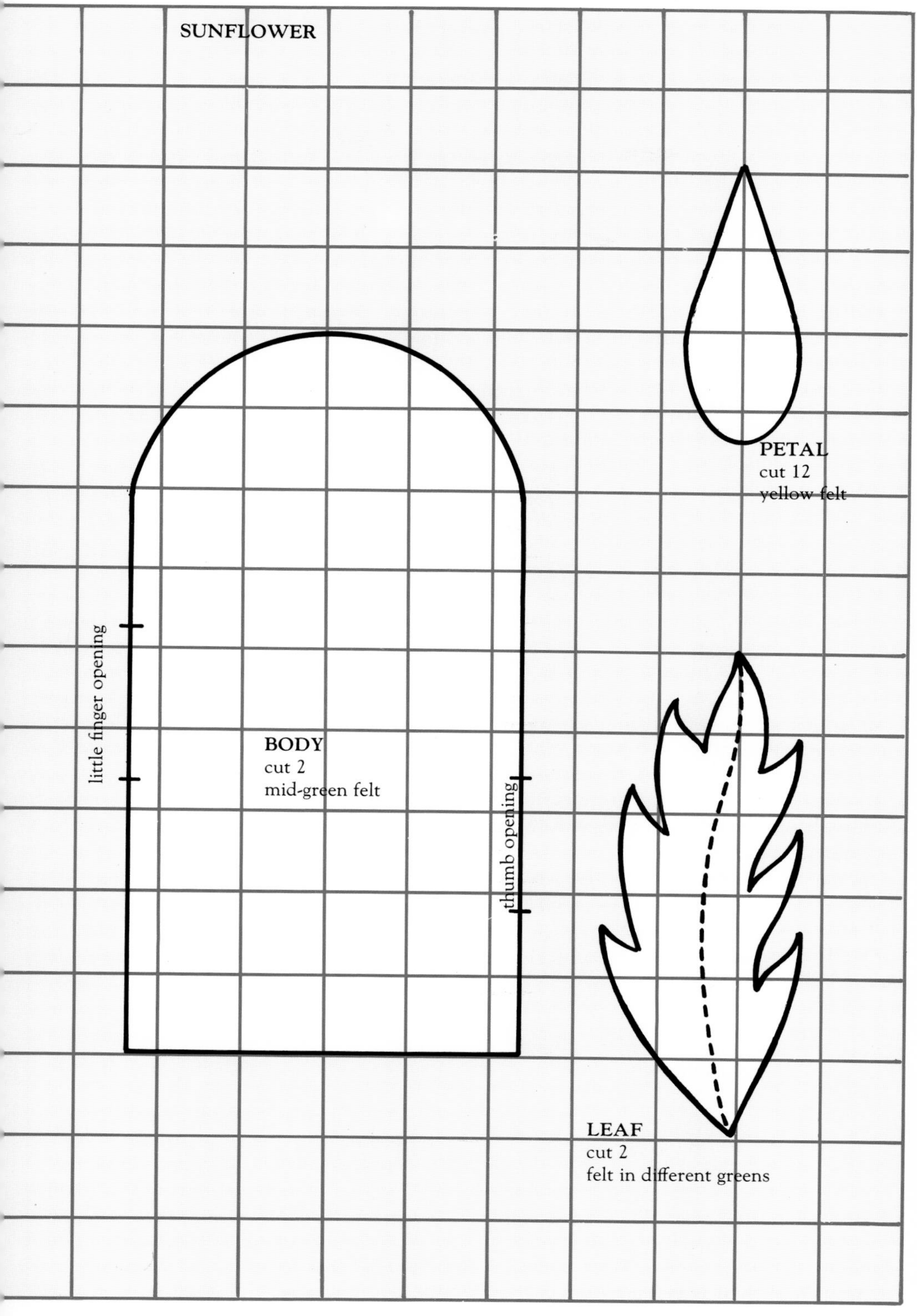

SUNFLOWER

PETAL
cut 12
yellow felt

little finger opening

BODY
cut 2
mid-green felt

thumb opening

LEAF
cut 2
felt in different greens

The Pied Piper

You can re-create the well-loved story of the Pied Piper of Hamelin with this colourful glove puppet and his pompon rats. The Piper's head is made of modelling clay.

Materials
For the Pied Piper
Small cardboard roll, or some thin card
Modelling clay (the size of a tennis ball)
Friable material such as sand, sawdust or
  breadcrumbs for hair
Red fabric: 2 pieces each 11 × 5½in
  (28 × 14cm), 1 piece 14¼ × 8¾in
  (36 × 22cm)
Yellow fabric: 2 pieces each 11in (28cm)
  square, 1 piece 14¼ × 8¾in (36 × 22cm)
12in (30cm) piece of green felt
Square of beige or flesh-pink felt
  sufficient to cut 4 thumb shapes
9 × 7½in (23 × 19cm) piece of yellow felt
Red and yellow felt strips
Lengths of narrow and wide red and
  yellow ribbon
Small piece of wood, such as a cocktail
  stick, for the pipe

For the rats
Grey, black, brown and pink wool
Black sewing thread
Scraps of yellow paper and pink felt

Making the Pied Piper
Head
1 If you cannot find a cardboard roll of a suitable size, make a roll from thin card which will fit, not too tightly, around your index finger, and which is the same length as your finger. Secure it with strong glue or rubber bands.

2 Covering the top of this tube and leaving about 1¼in (3cm) of tube clear at the bottom as a neck, make a head shape out of modelling clay. A head is roughly egg-shaped, narrower at the chin and tilted back at the crown. Hollow the cheeks slightly if you want a hungry look.

3 Add to the head a triangular nose and small sausages of modelling clay to create the brow ridges, lips and chin. Use modelling tools or the handle of an old teaspoon to smooth the joins and to help make the features.

4 Flatten very small spheres of clay as eyes and place them below the brows, pushing in the centre with a pencil point to form the pupils. Add tiny flattened sausages of clay as eyelids and, with your modelling tool, make strong hollows under the eyes. Add semicircular pieces of clay as ears, pushing them into shape. If you find this difficult, it helps to look closely at someone and copy their face, especially in the placing of features. Eyes, brows and nose are surprisingly low on the head, and the tops of the ears are roughly level with the eyes.

Heads modelled from clay can be used to caricature real people. You could make a pop group, a football team, your friends and neighbours, or even some politicians, as well as a fairy-tale character like mine.

The clothes worn by this Pied Piper puppet can be made as elaborate as you wish. You can make them in the same way as a conventional glove puppet as here, or use a simple circle of cloth with a hole in the centre.

The stages of modelling the head in clay.

5 Leave the head until it is completely dry and then paint it in any way you wish. If you want the hair to show, you can paint it, or cover the hair area with glue and then dip the head in any crumbly friable hair-coloured material.

Tunic

6 Hem each of the 11 × 5½in (28 × 14cm) pieces of red fabric down one long edge only. Place these 2 pieces right sides together so that the raw long edges match and stitch together down the raw edges only, leaving a 2in (5cm) opening 1¼in (3cm) down from the top to form the armhole.

7 Place the two 11in (28cm) square pieces of yellow fabric right sides together and stitch together down 2 opposite sides leaving, in the same way, a 2in (5cm) opening 1¼in (3cm) down from the top at each side.

8 Put the red half-tunic over one side of the yellow tunic so that all right sides are outwards, the armholes of the red and yellow sections match on one side, and the red fabric covers half of the yellow fabric at the back and front. Hem the top edges together, so neatening and also joining the red and yellow pieces together. Hem the bottom edges of the red and yellow fabric separately.

9 Trace and cut out the pattern for the arm shapes. Cut 4 arm shapes in felt. Place them together in pairs and firmly oversew together around the complete curved edge, leaving the straight edge open. Insert the arms into the armholes, matching the 2in (5cm) straight edges of the arms to the 2in (5cm) openings left in the side seams. Sew the arms into the armholes, catching down both the red

42

and yellow fabric into the seam at one side of the tunic, but only the yellow fabric at the other.

10 Run a gathering thread around the top neck edge of the tunic and draw it tightly around the neck of the puppet, tying it into place and sticking if preferred.

Cloak
11 Take the 2 pieces of $14\frac{1}{4} \times 8\frac{3}{4}$in (36 × 22cm) fabric, one red, one yellow, place them right sides together and seam together down one long edge. Hem the remaining 2 long sides. Cut rough zigzags along the bottom edge of the cloak.

12 Turn a wide hem on to the wrong side along the top edge and stitch it to form a casing for the ribbon. Thread the casing with ribbon or ribbons and gather and tie the cloak around the puppet's neck.

13 Stitch lengths of ribbon and strips of hemmed left-over fabric to the centre back neck of the cloak for decoration.

Hat
14 Cut one short edge of the piece of yellow felt into a deep jagged pattern. Stick the other short edge around the crown of the head, allowing the felt to form a soft cylinder. Plait strips of red and yellow felt and stick around the head where the hat is attached.

Pipe
15 If the stick for the pipe has sharp ends, rub them off with sandpaper, then paint the stick gold, adding spots to represent the holes. Stitch the pipe firmly to one of the puppet's hands.

To give a soft, natural-looking finish to the Pied Piper's face, use poster paints diluted with a lot of water. A very fine paintbrush brings out the details in the eyes.

Place the red half-tunic over one side of the yellow tunic, matching the armholes.

Gather the top of the tunic around the neck of the puppet.

Rats

16 Tie some black sewing thread tightly around the centre of a bundle of 1¼in (3cm) lengths of rat-coloured yarn to make a pompon. Plait three 4¾in (12cm) lengths of pink yarn and tie at the end to form a tail. Alternatively, make 4½in (11cm) lengths of twisted cord. Sew to the back of the rat. Cut and stick on diamond-shaped paper eyes in yellow with a black centre drawn on, and a pink circular felt nose. Tie to the middle of the rat a length of black sewing cotton long enough to go off stage when the rat is in the scene.

Fabric measurements for tunic and cloak

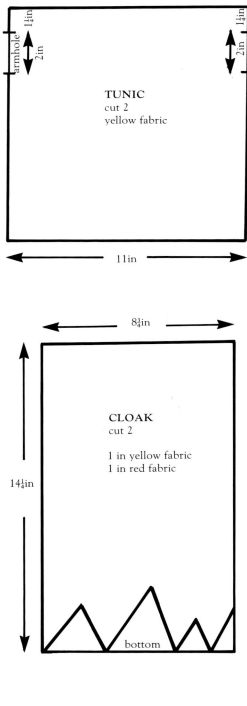

TUNIC
cut 2
yellow fabric

armhole

1¼in

2in

1¼in

2in

11in

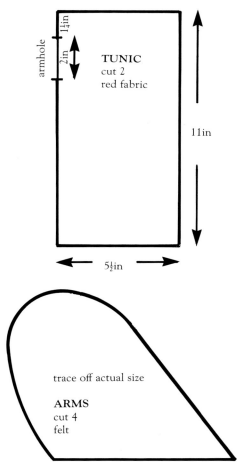

armhole

1¼in

2in

TUNIC
cut 2
red fabric

11in

5½in

trace off actual size

ARMS
cut 4
felt

8¾in

CLOAK
cut 2

1 in yellow fabric
1 in red fabric

14¼in

bottom

Tie sewing thread around a bundle of yarn lengths to make the pompon rats.

Rats on stage
As your audience arrives, the scene is set with the rats dotted about the stage eating things and up to all sorts of ratty no-good. When the play begins and the characters enter, helpers can pull the invisible lines from off-stage and the rats will appear to scamper away. They can all be pulled along together when they follow the Piper.

Jungle friend

What a lot of fun you are going to have with this tiger hand-puppet! The 'tigery' face is achieved by using tiger-striped fur fabric – there really is no substitute.

Materials

12in (30cm) of 54in (137cm)-wide tiger-
   striped fur fabric
8in (20cm) of 60in (150cm)-wide oatmeal
   close pile fur fabric
8in (20cm) of 54in (137cm)-wide white
   wild animal fur fabric
12in (30cm) of 36in (90cm)-wide lining
   fabric
6in (15cm) square of black felt
Two $\frac{1}{2}$in (12mm) amber toy eyes
Washable polyester toy filling

Preparation

1 Draw a pattern from the graph pattern
on page 48, on squared paper. Put in all
marks, words and numerals. Cut out the
pattern pieces.

2 From the striped fur fabric, cut 2
bodies on the fold, 2 upper faces, 2 back
heads and 2 ears. Cut also a strip $8\frac{3}{4} \times 2\frac{1}{2}$in
(22 × 6cm) for the tail.

3 From the white fur fabric, cut 2 lower
faces. From the close pile fur fabric, cut 1
muzzle and 2 ears.

4 From the lining, cut 2 bodies on the
fold. From felt, cut 2 irises, 1 nose and
mouth.

IRIS
cut 2
black felt

trace off actual size

NOSE AND MOUTH
cut 1   black felt

Making the tiger

5 Fold the tail lengthways in half and
stitch the long edges together and across
the lower end. Turn right side out and
baste to the lower edge of one body piece
at the centre. (This will be the back.)

6 Stitch the lining bodies together B–A–
A–B and turn right side out. Stitch the
fur bodies together A–B, slip the lining
inside the fur body and stitch together
around the lower edges, matching points
B and leaving a 4in (10cm) opening. Turn
and slip stitch the opening closed.

Stitch the upper
faces together.

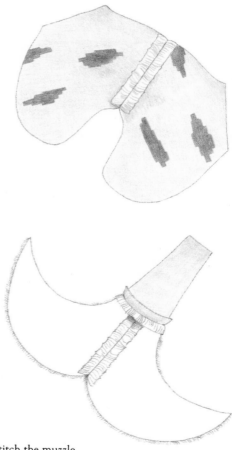

Stitch the muzzle
to the lower faces.

1 square = 1in (2.5cm)

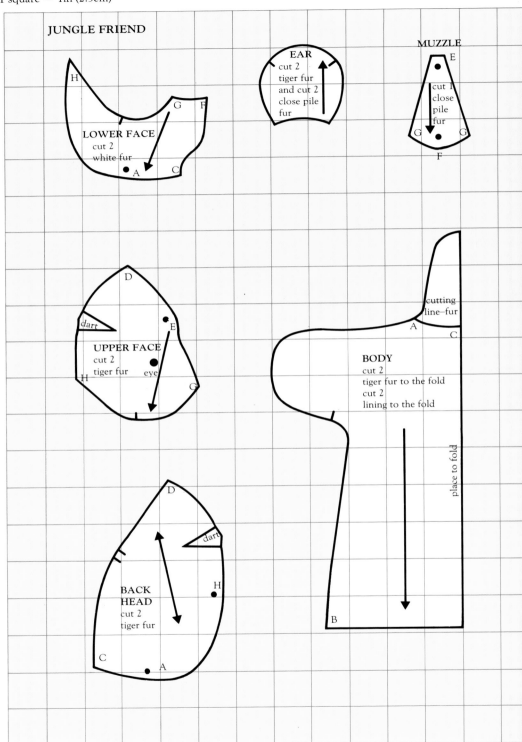

JUNGLE FRIEND

EAR
cut 2
tiger fur
and cut 2
close pile
fur

MUZZLE
E
cut 1
close
pile
fur
G   G
F

H
G   F
LOWER FACE
cut 2
white fur
● A   C

D
dart
E
UPPER FACE
cut 2
tiger fur   eye
H
G

cutting
line–fur
A
C

BODY
cut 2
tiger fur to the fold
cut 2
lining to the fold

place to fold

D
dart
BACK
HEAD
cut 2
tiger fur
H

C
● A

B

7 Slip your hand inside the body and pin the fur and lining together at the 'neck', matching A and C. Hand sew the raw edge of the fur to the lining.

8 Make tiny holes at the eye positions on the upper faces, then stitch the upper faces together D–E. Stitch the back heads together C–D. Stitch the darts.

9 Stitch the lower faces together C–F. Stitch the muzzle to the lower faces G–F–G.

10 Stitch the lower faces and muzzle to the upper face H–G–E–G–H, hand sewing the G–E–G part of the seam. Stitch each tiger-striped ear to a close pile ear around the notched edges. Turn right side out and baste the raw edges together.

11 Baste the ears to the top of the upper faces 2½in (6cm) apart, with the close pile fur ears facing the face. Stitch the back head to the face A–H–D–H–A. Turn right side out.

12 Make tiny holes in the centre of the irises. Insert the stalk of the eyes through the holes, then fix in position to the upper face.

13 Stuff the head around the outer edges, place the end of a thick pen or paintbrush handle inside centrally and continue stuffing firmly. Remove the pen and turn under ¼in (6mm) on the lower edges.

14 Slip your hand into the body and insert a finger in the top of the lining. Place the head on top facing forward and pin the turned-under edge ¼in (6mm) below the raw fur edge, matching A and C. Hand sew in place.

15 Pin the nose and mouth to the face with the top edge level with the lower edge of the muzzle. Hand sew in place.

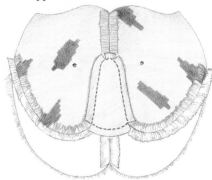

Stitch the lower faces and muzzle to the upper face.

Push the eye stalk through felt, then through face.

Slip your hand into the body, with forefinger in the lining.

49

THREE

Knitted puppets

Playful pig

Pigs are always popular with children and this hand puppet will be no exception. Quick and easy to knit in stocking stitch, he'll be ready to play in no time.

Materials
About 60g of pink Chunky knitting yarn
1 pair of 6½mm (No 3) knitting needles
2 small and 2 medium shiny round black
  buttons
Scrap of washable toy stuffing

Making the pig
Main body
Cast on 36 sts.
Work 2 rows of k1, p1 rib.
Change to st st and work straight until work measures 12in (30cm), ending with a p row. Mark the middle of the row.
Next row: K2 tog, k to 2 sts before the middle, k2 tog through back of sts, k2 tog, k to 2 sts before the end, k last 2 sts tog through back of sts.
Next row: P.
Rep these 2 rows until 20 sts rem.
Work 9 more rows, so ending with a p row.
Next row: K2 tog all across the row (10 sts rem).
Next row: P2 tog all across the row (5 sts rem).
Run a thread through these sts and pull them tight, then use this thread to seam the two sides of the knitting evenly together to form the underneath seam of the puppet.

Ears (make 2)
Cast on 10 sts.
Work 8 rows of st st.
Cont in st st, work 2 sts tog at each end of the next, then every alternate row until 2 sts rem.
Work 2 sts tog and fasten off.

Finishing
Flatten the end of the pig's nose into a typical snout shape and sew this shape into position through the 2 layers of knitting. Sew on the larger buttons as nostrils.

Sew on the ears by their cast-on edges at an angle just behind the shaped knitting of the face. Catch down the front edges of the ears in one place to give the piggy angle and shape. Sew on the smaller buttons for eyes at the sides of the head under the points of the ears, which, being stocking stitch, will curl up naturally. Push the stuffing to the front of the nose so that it keeps its round shape.

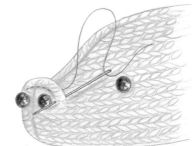

Flatten the nose into a snout shape and sew into position.

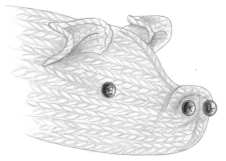

Sew on the ears and catch down at the front edges to give the correct shape.

Story-time finger puppets

With these finger puppets, you can re-enact the story of the White Knight and the Black Knight doing battle over the Princess imprisoned in the dragon's lair.

Materials
Small quantities of double knitting yarn in the chosen colours for each character
Scraps of contrast yarn for detail and embroidery
1 pair of 4mm (No 8) knitting needles
Very small quantity of toy stuffing or equivalent

Making the puppets
All the finger puppets are based on the same basic pattern which follows. The different characters are worked in the colours and detail given after the basic pattern. Instructions for making up and decorating the puppets are given at the end of all the knitting instructions.

Basic body shape
Cast on 14 sts and work 4 rows in k1, p1 rib.
Change to st st starting with a k row, and work 16 rows.
Next row: K2 tog 7 times (7 sts rem).
Next row: P1, p2 tog 3 times.
Run a thread through rem 4 sts.

White Knight: Make the basic body shape, casting on and working rib and first 10 rows of st st in white, then work 4 rows pink and complete in white.

Black Knight: Work as for the White Knight, but in black and pink instead of white and pink.

Princess: Work as for the White Knight, but in blue and pink instead of white and pink.

Dragon: Make the basic body shape in green.
Nose: Cast on 8 sts in green and work 4 rows in st st.
Next row: K2 tog 4 times.
Run a thread through rem 4 sts.

Work straight stitches for the features of the Knights and the Princess.

For the dragon's and horses' eyes, embroider a detached chain stitch with a centre.

White horse: Make the basic body shape in white, plus a white nose as given for dragon.

Black horse: Make the basic body shape in black, plus a black nose as given for dragon.

Making up the puppets

Make up each finger puppet by using the gathering thread to join the back seam, matching any colours. Seam the noses of the dragon and horses in the same way, stuff and attach immediately below the top of each puppet.

Knights: Sew on hair and features, and embroider a motif on the front. Sew a matching tassel on the helmet top.

Princess: Sew on yellow hair, tied in bows. Embroider features and add a cord at the waist.

Dragon: Embroider yellow and red eyes, a green fringed mane, a small white fringe as teeth, and red and yellow cut fringes as flames.

Horses: Embroider eyes and nostrils and make loops of buttonhole stitches for the ears. Embroider a cut fringe for the mane and sew on a bridle and reins in a contrast colour.

Fire-breathing dragon

With his sharp teeth, fearsome eyes and fiery breath, this dragon is quite spectacular. He is knitted from lots of different strands of yarn in mixed colours.

Materials

About 400g of all kinds of knitting yarns, brushed or plain, metallic or fashion, in blues and greens as well as some red, yellow, orange, white and black
1 pair of 10mm (No 000) and 1 pair of 5mm (No 6) knitting needles
Small sequins and beads for eyes
Large pointed sequins for teeth
2 large oval sequins for nostrils
Very small amounts of stuffing

Main body piece

Using the 10mm needles and 7 strands of yarn together in mixed colours, cast on 24 sts.
K 2 rows.
Change to st st and work 2 rows.
Work the very open rows on the dragon's body as follows:
* K 1 row, winding the yarn 3 times around the needle instead of once on every st.
P the next row, working each st through only 1 of the 3 loops around the needle from the previous row, and allowing the other 2 loops to fall from the needle.
K 1 row.
P 1 row *.
Rep from * to * once more.
Change to st st and work straight until work measures 20in (50cm), ending with a p row. N.B. You can continue your st st in any combination of colours you wish, perhaps adding areas of other colours such as the mixture of blues under the chin.

Top jaw

Next row: K2 tog, k8, k2 tog, then turn and work on these sts only, working 2 sts tog at each end of every 3rd row until 4 sts rem.
Cast off.

Bottom jaw

Return to the rem 12 sts and rejoin the yarns to the work at the inside edge.
Next row: K2 tog, k8, k2 tog, then turn and work on these sts only, working 2 sts tog at each end of every 3rd row until 4 sts rem.
Cast off.
Fold the work in half and seam the 2 sides tog to form the side seam of the puppet, leaving the shaped and cast-off edges of the mouth unseamed.

Mouth lining

Using the 10mm needles and about 7 strands of red, yellow and black yarn, cast on 4 sts.

These spectacular puppets are great fun to make and can be any size, colour or stitch pattern which is appropriate to the creature. They can be as long as you like, either just covering the hand or going up one arm, round the neck and back down to the other hand – an anaconda, perhaps. You can decorate them with any materials you have available and add any appropriate ears, tails or accessories.

Work in st st, starting with a k row, and inc 1 st at each end of every 3rd row until there are 12 sts.
Work 2 rows.
Continue in st st and work 2 tog at each end of the next then every foll 3rd row until there are 4 sts.
Cast off.

Sew the lining into the dragon's mouth, doubling it at the centre which becomes the back of the mouth and matching the shape of the top and bottom jaws. Sew an open-ended thumb shape through the bottom jaw to accommodate the operator's thumb.

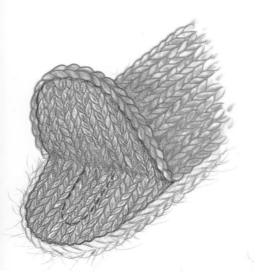

Sew the lining into the mouth and sew a thumb shape through the bottom jaw.

Tongue

Using 10mm needles and about 7 strands of yellow and orange yarn, cast on 44 sts.
1st row: Cast off 22 sts, k rem 22 sts.
Next row: K the 22 sts, then cast on a further 10 sts.
Next row: Cast off 20 sts, k rem 12 sts.
Next row: K the 12 sts, then cast on a further 18 sts.
Cast off all 30 sts.
Sew the tongue by one end into the back of the mouth.

Eyes

Using 5mm needles and double yarn, 1 strand green, 1 strand blue, cast on 3 sts.
1st row: Work twice into every st in k.
Next row: P.
Rep these 2 rows once more (12 sts).
Cont in st st, work 4 more rows, then change to 2 strands of white and work 2 further rows.
Next row: K 2 sts tog all across the row.
Next row: P.
Rep these 2 rows once more, then run a thread through the remaining 3 sts.
Stuff each eye to form a hemisphere and sew on to the top of the head with the white towards the front. Embroider a black circle in the centre of the white and sew a ring of beads around it. Embroider black eyelashes.

Sew on the features and embroider a line of fringing down the centre back.

Finishing

Sew on the pointed sequins all around the edge of the top jaw as teeth and sew on the oval sequins as nostrils. Embroider a line of fringing down the centre back.

Make and attach a twisted cord or plaited tail and sew a large multicoloured pompon to the free end.

FOUR

String puppets

Round felt man

Children will love this fat and cheerful little man, who can dance and move his arms most convincingly. He is easy to operate with three strings on a single stick.

Materials
Two 6in (15cm) squares of felt, one blue and one green
Two 4in (10cm) squares of orange felt
Small pieces of brown felt and a scrap of red felt
3 large red buttons
2 small blue buttons
Fourteen 1½in (3.5cm) diameter orange craft pompons
Two 1½in (3.5cm) diameter brown craft pompons
Two 2in (5cm) diameter brown craft pompons
Small quantity of toy stuffing
Strong black thread
12in (30cm) length of dowelling or cane

Preparation
1 With a pair of compasses, draw a circle 5¾in (14.5cm) in diameter for the body shape and a circle 3½in (9cm) in diameter for the head shape.

2 Using these patterns, cut 2 large felt circles for the body, 1 in green and 1 in blue. Cut 2 small orange felt circles for the head. Trace the patterns for the front and back hair and cut out in brown felt. Also cut a small mouth shape in red felt.

Making the felt man
3 Stitch together the 2 body circles and lightly stuff. Stitch together the 2 head circles and lightly stuff. Sew the head to the body so that it overlaps the body slightly at the front. Sew on the back and front hair pieces so that they match at the sides and the top curve of the hair matches that of the head.

4 For each leg, knot the end of a length of strong thread. Then, using a long sewing needle, thread 1 large brown and 4 orange pompons on to the thread. Firmly stitch the threaded pompons to the bottom of the body. Make and attach the arms in the same way, but use a smaller brown pompon and only 3 orange pompons.

5 Sew on the small blue buttons as eyes and the red buttons down the centre of the body as the puppet's buttons. Stick on the red felt mouth.

Variations
These puppets are ideal for human figures and can be in any colour, pattern and fabric, with square or oval bodies. The craft pompons are available in all sorts of colours so that you can create a whole range of characters. They are ideal for groups of puppets, perhaps for a crowd scene, as they move convincingly and can wave their arms about. If you enjoy decorating the puppets, the button idea can be elaborated upon and you could create, for example, sequined dancers, or a Pearly King and Queen. These puppets could also be dressed in simple baggy clothes which do not inhibit their movements, for example, gathered skirts or baggy dungarees.

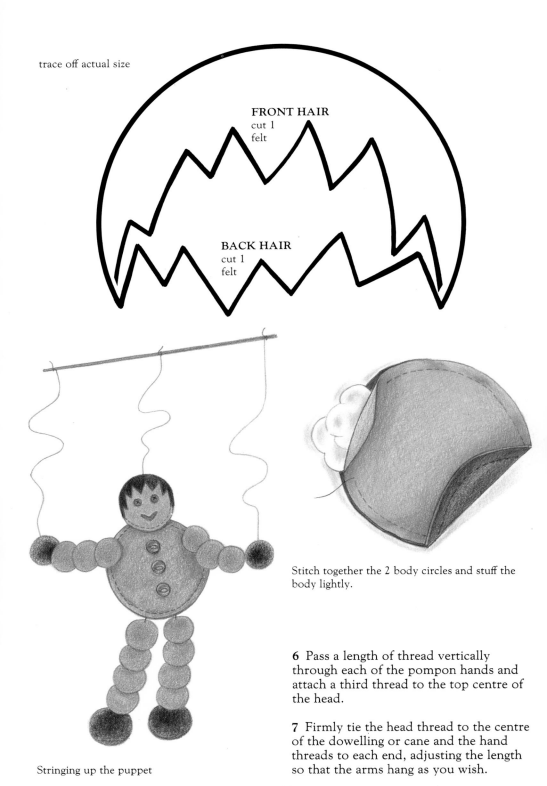

trace off actual size

FRONT HAIR
cut 1
felt

BACK HAIR
cut 1
felt

Stitch together the 2 body circles and stuff the body lightly.

6 Pass a length of thread vertically through each of the pompon hands and attach a third thread to the top centre of the head.

7 Firmly tie the head thread to the centre of the dowelling or cane and the hand threads to each end, adjusting the length so that the arms hang as you wish.

Stringing up the puppet

Ball birds

These birds can hop and prance on their spindly legs in a very engaging manner. They can be made of any lightweight balls or polystyrene craft balls.

Materials

(For each puppet)

2 lightweight balls, one smaller than the other

Small pieces of felt in chosen beak/foot colour

Scraps of black and white felt

Coloured wool or yarn

Strong black thread

Very small quantity of toy stuffing

Preparation

1 Trace the patterns for the foot pieces and the beak. Cut out in felt 4 foot pieces and 1 beak piece in the appropriate size.

Making the birds

2 Sew the beak piece into a cone, stuff, and glue open-ended to the centre of one side of the smaller ball. Cut out 2 small black and 2 very small white felt circles for the eyes. Stick the eyes to either side of the smaller ball, ensuring that they are symmetrical in relation to the beak.

3 Make a plait or twisted cord from the yarn between 10in (25cm) and 15¾in (40cm) long depending on the size of the bird. This length will pass through the body to make both legs.

These puppets are very easy to make. The trick lies in the choice of balls. They need to be light and pierceable – cheap balls in any toy shop fit the bill. You can also buy polystyrene balls and other shapes from crafts shops. Any puppet whose body is a suitable shape can be made in this way, but birds are ideal because they have round bodies, spindly legs and are simple in form. You could add felt or paper wings, tails made from paper or real feathers, and crests or eyelashes. You could also put objects such as felt fish in the beak, but take care that these are not too heavy or they will weight the bird down.

Threading the balls

A large sewing needle will go through sponge balls quite easily. Push gently and take care where the point comes out. On plastic balls with holes, you can use the existing holes for the legs. For the vertical operating thread, heat a needle carefully in a flame and it will melt the plastic and pass cleanly through it. The length of strong thread can then be threaded through these holes at top and bottom.

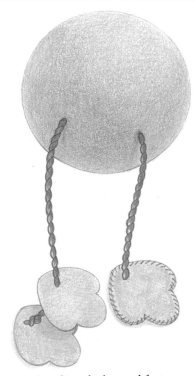

Attaching the legs and feet.

4 Knot one end of the cord or plait and, using a very large, long sewing needle, thread it up through a felt foot piece about ⅜in (1cm) from the back. Then thread it through the base of the larger ball at the leg position and down through the second felt foot piece. Knot the cord or plait off firmly.

5 Matching the shaping, sew another foot piece to the bottom of each of the feet, so concealing the knot.

6 Using a large sewing needle, knot a long piece of strong thread and take it vertically up through the larger 'body' ball and then through the smaller 'head' ball. Take care that this thread is properly vertical so that the legs are symmetrical at the bottom, and the eyes and beak are correctly positioned.

7 Make a looped knot in the top of the thread for the operator's finger.

Sew the beak piece into a cone and stuff.

BEAK
cut 1
felt

FEET
cut 4
felt

trace off actual size

LARGE VERSION

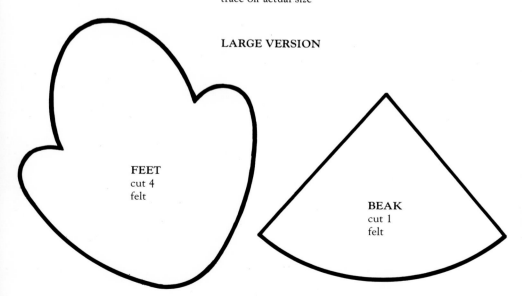

FEET
cut 4
felt

BEAK
cut 1
felt

Creeping caterpillar

This pompon caterpillar loops along in an amusingly life-like fashion. Quick to string together, he'll entertain young and old alike.

Materials
About 13 craft pompons in assorted colours
12in (30cm) length of dowelling or cane
Beads and scraps of black felt for eyes
Strong black thread

Making the caterpillar
1 Thread the craft pompons on to a length of the thread, using a long sewing needle and fastening off firmly at each end with knots.

2 Cut 2 equal threads about 18in (45cm) long and, in a similar way, thread one up through the middle of the first pompon, and the second up through a pompon a little over half-way along the caterpillar.

Tie the other end of each thread firmly to the dowelling or cane, ensuring that the threads are of equal length and hang vertically.

3 Glue very small circles of felt and beads as eyes to the sides of the first pompon, which becomes the head.

This caterpillar moves in a very realistic way, looping in the middle as many caterpillars do. Few other creatures, except perhaps snakes and eels, are this shape, and even they do not move in this distinctive way.
   Instead of using craft pompons you could make your own (see instructions on page 103 in Better Techniques) or use beads or any other threadable materials. The caterpillars could be any size; if made from your own woollen pompons, they would be especially large, but they could also be made of small beads and be very short.

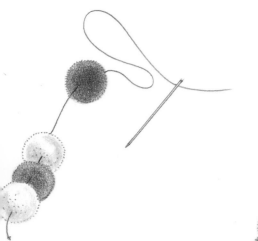

Thread the pompons on to a length of thread, using a long sewing needle.

Thread 1 string through the caterpillar's head, the other further along his body.

Ghost

This simple-to-make ghosty, as well as being a puppet, would be an ideal Hallowe'en decoration, and you could make lots – nasty and nice, cheerful and miserable.

Materials

Man's plain handkerchief or similar square of white fabric
2½in (6cm) diameter polystyrene ball
1 large and 2 small white beads
3 lengths of transparent nylon line, 8in (20cm), 10in (25cm) and 12in (30cm) long respectively
12in (30cm)-long fine cane or rod
Scraps of black felt

Making the ghost

1 Tie the large bead to one end of the longest nylon thread. Using a very long darning needle, draw the other end of the thread straight through the middle of the polystyrene ball so that the bead prevents the ball from falling off the end of the thread. Draw the same thread, with the needle, through the exact centre of the handkerchief and then tie the free end of the thread to the centre of the rod. The ball, covered by the handkerchief, now hangs from the centre of the rod and forms the head of the ghost.

Use different lengths of thread for the two 'arms' to make the ghost more interesting and attach them at different points. A long rod could hold more than one ghost and they could be as large or as small as you wish. Ghosts of different sizes attached to one rod across the back of a puppet scene would look as though they were the same size but different distances away. It would be fun to use luminous paint and to experiment with lighting the ghosts in an eerie way for your play.

2 Tie a smaller bead to the end of one of the shorter lengths of thread and draw the thread through one corner of the handkerchief. Again, the bead prevents the thread from pulling through. Tie the free end of the thread to one end of the rod. Do the same with the other bead and thread, about 4in (10cm) in from the opposite corner of the handkerchief. Tie the thread to the other end of the rod.

3 Cut 2 eye shapes and a mouth shape from the black felt and stick on to the handkerchief at the front of the head.

Stringing up the ghost.

Snake on a stick

This fascinating paper puppet is based on a traditional Chinese snake toy. The paper-folding process looks complicated, but is actually a familiar and simple way of making decorations.

Materials

Two 29½ × 1¼in (75 × 3cm) strips of coloured paper
Oval wooden bead
Scrap of strong thread or plastic strip for the tongue
Sequins, scraps of felt and/or beads for eyes
Transparent nylon thread
12in (30cm)-long stick

Making the snake

1 Place the 2 strips of paper at a perfect right angle to each other to form an 'L' shape and stick them together in this shape, making sure that the ends of the strips form a perfect square at the corner of the 'L'.

2 Take the underneath strip and fold it completely over the square at the bottom of the 'L', keeping the square as accurate as possible. Take the other strip and fold it over the first in the same way. Continue to repeat these 2 steps until the strips are all used up and you are left with a tightly folded square.

3 Taking care not to get glue on any other areas of the paper, stick the 2 end squares of the strips together. When the glue is dry, carefully pull the top and bottom glued squares away from one another and you will have an expanding strip like a concertina, which is the body of your snake.

4 Cut a fine strip of strong thread or plastic and make a slit at one end to form the forked tongue. Stick this into the hole at one side of the bead.

5 Stick on eyes made of sequins, beads and/or circular scraps of felt.

6 Drill a very small hole into the top of the bead as far as the centre and thread up through this a knotted 12in (30cm) length of transparent nylon thread, so that the head is hanging from this thread. Or, if you prefer, attach the thread by tying or gluing.

7 Stick the back of the head to one end of the folded paper body.

8 Tie the other end of the thread to the top of the operating stick and stick the other end of the paper body near the bottom of the stick.

These puppets sway about very realistically, but the technique is really only suitable for snakes. They could, however, be different sizes or colours, and could be decorated with sequins, glitter, drawn or painted motifs or any other form of elaborate trimming. Take care that the decoration is not too heavy as the snakes are fairly frail. On the other hand, unless they are very big, they need to be made of fine paper or the concertina-shaped body will be too stiff to move like a snake.

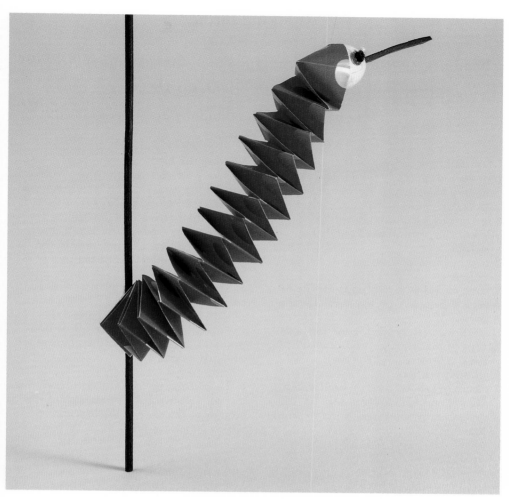

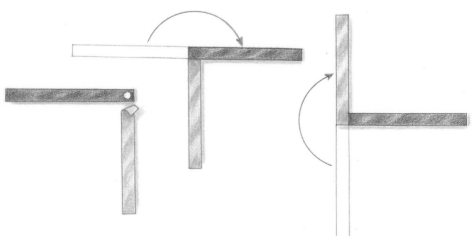

The stages of folding the paper strips to form the snake's body.

Walking birds

Waddling about in an ungainly fashion, these pompon birds are full of character. Use your brightest yarns, beads and feathers for this comical pair.

Materials

(For each puppet)

Stiff card sufficient to cut 2 each of the pompon circles

50g knitting yarn in body colour

30g knitting yarn in head and 'wing' colour

Small quantity of knitting yarn in leg colour

7 large round wooden beads for the neck

6 very large oval wooden beads for the toes

6 small wooden beads for the toe-nails

Scraps of black, white, and orange or dark yellow felt

Coloured feathers

2 pieces of garden cane or similar, 6in (15cm) and 12in (30cm) long

Transparent nylon thread such as fishing line

Preparation

1 Trace the pompon circles and cut 2 of each out of stiff card.

2 Make the body pompon on the larger card circles as shown on page 103 of the Better Techniques section. Use the yarn in the main body colour until the hole is about two-thirds filled. Change to the 'wing' colour and continue to bind evenly, using this colour until the first colour is completely covered and the hole filled.

3 Make the head pompon on the smaller card circles, using the head colour throughout.

Making the bird

4 Firmly attach a length of yarn to the tie around the centre of the body pompon. Thread the 7 neck beads on to this yarn so that the bottom one lies against the surface of the body, then firmly attach the other end of the neck yarn to the tie around the centre of the head pompon.

5 Make a 16in (40cm) plait or twisted cord for the legs, leaving 3 long strands of yarn free at each end. Thread this plait or cord through the centre of the body pompon, arranging it so that the legs are of equal length.

6 Thread a large oval wooden bead, then a small wooden bead on to each of the strands at the ends of the legs and secure with a large firm knot.

7 Trace the pattern for the beak shape and cut out in orange or dark yellow felt. Sew the 2 straight edges together to form a cone and stick firmly to the front of the head. For the eyes, cut 2 small black circles and 2 very small white circles in felt, then stick to each side of the head.

8 Glue the tail feathers firmly into the back of the body pompon.

9 Tie the shorter piece of cane firmly by its centre to a point on the longer cane approximately 5in (12.5cm) from one end. This will become the front end of the cross frame.

10 With a piece of nylon thread approximately 19in (48cm) long, hang the body of the bird from the crossing point of the frame, securing the other end to the tie around the body pompon.

11 Ask someone to hold your puppet for you, or suspend it from a suitable shelf or chair, so that the bottom of the body is about 4in (10cm) from the floor and the legs appear too long. Now attach a nylon thread from the top of the head pompon to the front end of the longer piece of cane, so that the neck curves in a bird-like way.

12 Still supporting the puppet, now by 2 nylon threads, tie a similar thread to each leg approximately 2in (5cm) from the body. Tie each of these threads to the appropriate end of the shorter piece of cane so that each leg bends in a 'knee' and the feet are flat on the floor. The puppet will now walk happily if you use the frame to lift each leg in turn and move it forward.

As the stringing of these puppets is much simpler than that of a conventional 'human' marionette, they are less likely to get into a frustrating tangle. To avoid tangling, store them hanging from their frames or placed carefully in a box.

Their shape is perfect for bird characters like running ostriches, but you could consider other creatures such as two-legged dragons or dinosaurs. Try making a caterpillar from a row of pompons, each with a pair of legs, on a frame with lots of crosspieces. A cowboy, or any character who walks with bowed legs, is another possibility.

Threading on the beads for the bird's feet.

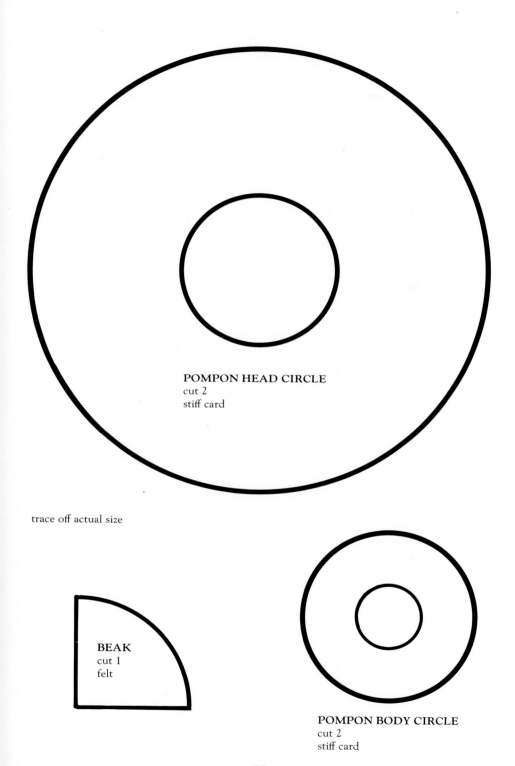

POMPON HEAD CIRCLE
cut 2
stiff card

trace off actual size

BEAK
cut 1
felt

POMPON BODY CIRCLE
cut 2
stiff card

FIVE

Rod puppets

Dancing girls

A dish mop, a wooden spoon and some oddments of fabric are all you need to create these dancing girls which twirl gracefully at the twist of a handle.

Materials
For the dish mop puppet
A dish mop
Dye in a natural hair colour
16in (40.5cm) diameter circle of fabric, polythene or paper
8 large oval beads
5½in (14cm) square scrap of fabric
Ribbon, lace and strong thread, plus other decorative materials of choice
2¼in (5.5cm) diameter circle of thin beige card

For the wooden spoon puppet
A wooden spoon
Thick yellow yarn
Decorative beads
Fabric, large oval beads, strong thread and trimmings as for dish mop puppet

Preparation for dish mop puppet
1 Using the dye according to the manufacturer's instructions, dye the dishmop strands for coloured 'hair'.

Making both puppets
2 Stitch lace or ribbon around the circumference of the 16in (40.5cm) circle of fabric. It is not necessary to hem the fabric as it will not fray too much when cut in a circle. Paper or polythene circles could have trim stuck on to them.

3 Make a small hole exactly in the centre of the 16in (40.5cm) circle and push the handle of the dish mop or spoon through it until it is about ¾in (2cm) below the 'hair' or the bowl of the spoon. Using fabric glue and thread, wire or wire bag closures, stick and tie the centre of the fabric firmly around the handle on the underside so that it will not show.

Tie the centre of the dress around the handle from the underside.

Gather the dress at the waist.

4 Run a gathering thread in a 3in (7.5cm) diameter circle around the centre of the fabric, i.e. 1½in (4cm) away from the handle which will be in the middle. Pull this thread tight and secure it to form the waist.

5 Thread a length of very fine ribbon or strong thread straight through both sides of the fabric at the shoulders, so that it extends about 6in (15cm) at either side. To form the arms, thread 4 beads on to each of these 2 ribbon or thread lengths, tying the last one firmly to secure them.

Sew the top of each plait to the inside of the wooden spoon puppet's head-dress.

6 To make the apron, hem the square of fabric on 3 sides, leaving the top edge raw. Decorate the bottom edge with contrast ribbon or other trimmings such as embroidery, beads or braid.

As well as making attractive individual characters or dolls, these puppets look particularly good in groups. A dancing troupe is ideal because when the puppets are twirled their skirts behave especially well, and they can be given matching and toning costumes.

7 Gather the top edge of the apron square and stitch firmly to the centre of a long length of ribbon. Tie this around the waist, leaving the long ends free or tying them into a bow.

Finishing the dish mop puppet
8 Draw a simple face on to the circle of card and stick it to the flattened front of the mop.

Finishing the wooden spoon puppet
9 Cut strands of thick yellow yarn and stick them evenly to the top of the convex side of the spoon bowl to form a front hair-line and parting. Wind a thick twist or plait of the yarn into a hair-piece shape and stick into the concave side of the spoon bowl to form the back of the hair.

10 Make a head-dress by stitching together lengths of ribbon and broderie anglaise to form a 'crown'. Make plaits from the yellow yarn, tying them with bows of thin ribbon. Sew the top of each plait to the inside of the head-dress so that they hang at each side. Catch the head-dress down with a few stitches to the yarn glued to the spoon.

11 Thread decorative beads on to a short thread and tie firmly around the neck as a necklace.

12 Draw a simple face on the convex side of the spoon bowl.

Pop-up baby

This puppet pops in and out of its cylindrical base when you move the rod up and down. Young children, especially, love the element of surprise as the baby plays peep-bo.

Materials

5½in (14cm)-long tube of card 3½in (9cm)
   in diameter, or a 5½ × 11¾in (14 × 30cm)
   piece of card
15¾in (40cm) length of rod, cane or
   dowelling
2in (5cm) diameter polystyrene craft ball
13¾ × 11¾in (35 × 30cm) piece of pink
   jersey fabric plus an additional tiny
   scrap for nose
8in (20cm) square of white cotton fabric
11¾in (30cm) of wide pink broderie
   anglaise edging
36½in (93cm) of narrow pink broderie
   anglaise edging
19¾in (50cm) of narrow pink velvet
   ribbon
19¾in (50cm) of white lace edging
Scrap of dark pink felt
Small quantity of blue, black, red and
   white embroidery threads
3½in (9cm) diameter circle of card for base
   of body cylinder

Preparation

1 If necessary, roll and stick the card
into a tube 5½in (14cm) long with a
diameter of 3½in (9cm).

2 Firmly push the rod into the centre of
one side of the polystyrene craft ball and
stick into position.

Making the baby

3 Take the pink jersey fabric and stitch
the two 13¾in (35cm) edges together to
form a cylinder of fabric which will
tightly cover the cylinder of card. Place
the card cylinder inside the fabric
cylinder so that the fabric overlaps the
card by ⅜in (1cm) at the bottom, with the
remainder of the fabric cylinder above
the top of the card. Turn the ⅜in (1cm)
fabric overlap up inside the card and
stick in place.

4 Gather the top raw edge of the fabric
as tightly as possible and fasten off. Push
the ball on the rod up the card and fabric
cylinder so that it is tight against the
gathered top and vertical within the
cylinder. Run a tight gathering thread
around the fabric immediately below the
ball and fasten off to form the baby's
neck and head.

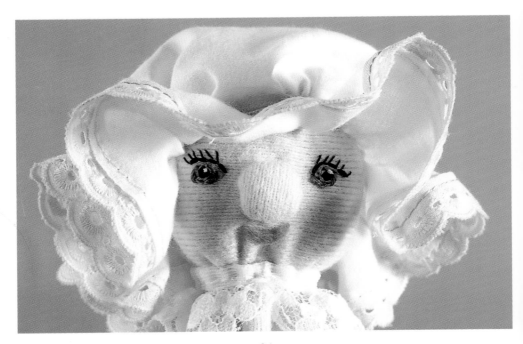

84

Cover the card cylinder with the fabric cylinder. Gather the fabric around the polystyrene ball and rod to form the head and neck.

To gather the mob cap, run a circle of thread around the fabric and pull up.

5 Cut an 8in (20cm) diameter circle from the white cotton fabric. Stitch on narrow pink broderie anglaise around the outer edge. Run a circle of gathering thread around the fabric circle 1¼in (3cm) in from the edge. Gather tightly enough to fit the baby's head as a mob cap and stitch evenly on to the head. Trim around the gathering thread with narrow pink velvet ribbon.

6 Decorate the cylinder of fabric with sewn-on lengths of wide and narrow pink broderie anglaise, pink velvet ribbon and white lace. Round off each end of the remaining white lace into a collar shape, then gather and sew into place around the neck.

Finishing
7 Cut a ¾in (2cm) circle from the scrap of pink jersey fabric. Run a gathering thread all around the edge and pull tight, drawing the raw edges in. Sew the resulting button shape to the centre of the face to form the nose.

8 Cut out and stick on a mouth in dark pink felt. Embroider blue eyes with black centres and lashes. Add a white dot in the centre of each eye and a red dot at the inner corner to give expression.

9 Using a damp red crayon, gently pencil in colour to the cheeks.

10 To prevent the puppet's body from dropping down the stick, you will need to add a card base to the cylinder. In the centre of the card circle, cut a hole marginally smaller than the diameter of the rod. Push the rod down through the hole and wedge the card circle into the base of the body cylinder.

Because these puppets are such a simple concept, as well as being one of the oldest forms of toy, almost any character can be made in this way. You could try a bear, a clown, a burglar or a Jack-in-the-Box. Any creature that lives in a hole, such as a rabbit, a gopher, a gerbil or a mole, would be fun, as would a snake in a basket or even some of Ali Baba's forty thieves in jars.

Old man and old woman

These rod puppets have papier mâché heads and their arms are operated on canes. Almost life-size, the old man and the old woman are intriguingly realistic.

Materials
(For each puppet)
A balloon
Newspaper
Wallpaper paste
Cardboard egg-box
Small amount of tissue paper or kitchen paper
Few sheets of plain white paper
Half of a broomstick handle
Scraps of sheepskin or white fur fabric for old man
Thick grey, black and white knitting wool for old woman
Child-sized wire coat-hanger
Child's old shirt or blouse and a scarf
Optional beads for old woman
Piece of flesh-coloured felt large enough for 4 hand shapes
Small quantity of wadding
2 thin canes

Making the puppets
Papier mâché head
1 Blow up the balloon to about three-quarters the size of a human head. Tear the newspaper into small pieces and, using the wallpaper paste, glue the pieces on to the balloon in a fairly thin layer. Leave to dry somewhere warm like an airing cupboard for about 24 hours. You might find it easiest to hang the balloon up by its neck, using a clothes peg tied to a rail.

2 Repeat the layering process 3 or 4 more times. It is useful to do alternate layers in coloured newsprint if available, so that you can see where you have worked.

3 To make the nose, cut one of the 'bumps' from the egg-box and stick it in position on the dry head, remembering that people's noses are surprisingly low down on their faces. Make small sausage shapes of screwed-up tissue paper or kitchen paper and stick them on to make the ridges of the prominent brows and the bridge of the nose. Make the chin in the same way or use another egg-box 'bump'. Apply a fresh layer of newspaper pieces over these features with the wallpaper paste and allow to dry.

4 Drying each layer for at least a day before applying the next, add about 2 more layers, finishing when the papier mâché of the head is strong but not too thick, because this will make it very heavy. Work the last 2 layers in small pieces of plain white paper, as this is easier to paint than the dark newsprint.

5 Burst the balloon and remove it. Widen the hole at the bottom of the head so that the broomstick is a firm push fit. Apply a thick layer of PVA glue to the very top of the broomstick, then push the stick into the neck so that the head rests gently on the top of it, ensuring that the stick is vertical with the head at a realistic angle. Apply a generous ring of PVA glue around the junction between the stick and the head, and allow the glue to dry.

6 Paint the head and the features in realistic colours.

Hair

7 To make the old man's hair, cut sheepskin pieces or white fur fabric to shape and glue on to the head.

8 To make the old woman's hair, cut lengths of wool about twice the head's circumference, mixing white, grey and black strands. Allowing each glued line of hair to dry before applying the next, attach the wool in the following way: Draw 4 thick lines of PVA glue, 2 parallel at the centre parting and 1 to either side of these. Lay doubled lengths of wool across the lines of glue, sticking them by their centres in dense rows. When the hair is dry, style it into a bun and stitch firmly into place.

Dressing the puppets

9 Cut off the hook of the wire coat-hanger, leaving a 2in (5cm) stem. With adhesive tape, firmly attach the coat-hanger to the broomstick at shoulder level.

10 Hang the shirt or blouse on the coat-hanger. Hide the neck join with the scarf. Make a necklace of beads for the old woman, if required.

Hands

11 Trace the pattern for the hand shape. Cut 4 from felt and sew together in matching pairs. Lightly stuff with wadding and stitch finger shapes as shown. Sew the hands inside the shirt or blouse cuffs.

The papier mâché method of making puppets creates surprisingly realistic characters. You could add legs and trousers to the body, but you would need to make a hole in the back of the shirt for your hand, or have a very long rod to operate such a puppet. Other accessories could include a hat, a cloak or gloves.

12 Firmly stitch the end of a thin cane to each hand so that the arms can be animated by another operator, or by yourself with practice. If you wish to animate the old person on your own, you may prefer to stitch one arm into a realistic pose and move only one hand with a cane.

Form the features with egg-box 'bumps' and screwed-up paper.

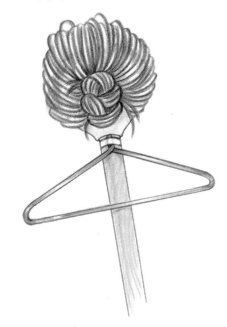

Attach a coat-hanger to the broomstick at shoulder level.

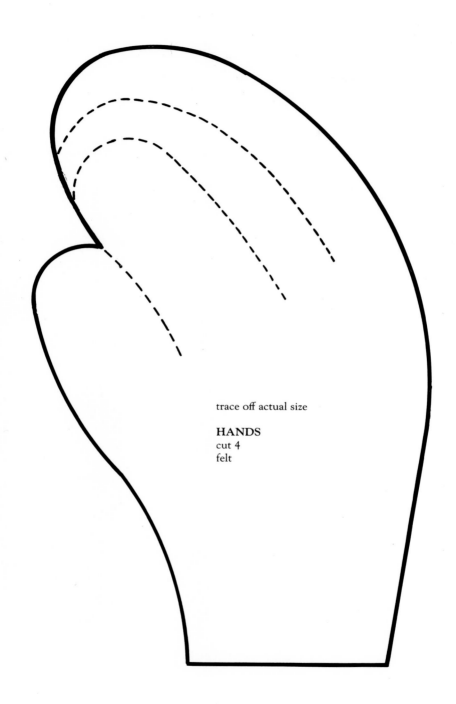

trace off actual size

HANDS
cut 4
felt

Punch and Judy rod puppet theatre

*Set up your own Punch and Judy show in this richly decorated
theatre. Sumptuous as it looks, it is easy to construct
from a sturdy cardboard box.*

Materials

A strong cardboard box with a lid or top
flaps

Additional strong card for 'wings' if
required

Decorative paper to cover and line the
box

Scraps of fabric for curtains at front and
back of the box

Ribbon for decoration

Thin card for puppets

Thin canes or rods at least the length of
the box

Making the theatre

1 If you are using the box upright, stick
or tape the lid or top of the box on
firmly. Using a craft knife, neatly cut out
the front, leaving about a fifth of the
height as a wall behind which the puppets
move, and also some card across the top
for strength. Alternatively, use the box
on its side and cut 2 of the flaps to form
the front wall and the top pelmet. Secure
with adhesive tape.

2 At each end of the box cut a vertical
slit up from the bottom, big enough for
the puppets to enter. Stagger them so
that one is nearer the front of the stage
than the other.

3 Line the floor and sides inside the box
stage with decorative paper and carefully
stick down, especially at the cut edges.

4 Cut card 'wings' and stick them on at
the sides of the stage. Alternatively, cut
these from the box side flaps.

5 Stick decorative paper all over the outside of the theatre box and 'wings', cutting it with a craft knife at the front and side openings, and covering the cut edges of the box.

6 Make stage curtains from pieces of hemmed fabric decorated with ribbon, long enough to go from top to bottom of the theatre. Pleat the fabric and stick it into position each side of the front opening. Add ribbon tie-backs. Staple a similar pleated curtain inside the back of the theatre.

7 Add a decorative strip across the top of the stage, using ribbon and paper cut with a scalloped edge.

Cut out the front of the box and slits at the sides. Add 'wings' to each side of the stage. The theatre illustrated measures 16in (40cm) wide, 11½in (29cm) high and 7½in (19cm) deep.

Making the puppets

8 Trace the 4 puppet shapes on to card and cut out. Paint on the features and details. Add a matchstick truncheon to the Policeman and a string of cut-out sausages to Toby the dog. Using adhesive tape, stick one end of a rod to the bottom of each puppet. Make sure it is low enough down to be well out of sight and parallel with the stage when the puppet is upright.

The box on which the theatre is based can be of any convenient size, but should preferably not be too deep from front to back or the puppets may be difficult to see.

Ideally a rod puppet theatre will have 2 operators and then characters can easily come in from each side or even at the front of the theatre. Any favourite story can be enacted and there can be a cast of thousands if you wish!

You can use figures cut from magazines or greetings cards or, of course, make up any characters of your own. Make sure that each puppet has a high enough base to enable it to be seen over the front wall of the theatre.

The theatre is more versatile if the backdrop is made from a series of painted card sheets, so that the scene can be changed during a play, or several different plays can be performed without the necessity of repainting the box.

Pleat fabric and trim with ribbon to make back and side stage curtains.

PUNCH

CROCODILE

trace off actual size

POLICEMAN

TOBY THE DOG

SAUSAGES

SIX

Better Techniques

❧

Everything you need to know to make successful puppets of all kinds is in this chapter. There is also a section on putting on a puppet show at home.

BASIC TOOLS AND EQUIPMENT

With the simplest of materials you can make all the puppets in this book and you will probably have most of the materials you need in your home. Apart from fabrics, paper, card and an assortment of kitchen discards, only very few tools are needed. Cutting tools are, of course, essential. You will also need paper with which to make patterns, some drawing implements, adhesives, the usual sewing aids, and a variety of paints and paintbrushes.

Scissors

You will need three pairs of scissors. First, dressmaking scissors with sharp blades and pointed tips for cutting fabrics. A small pair of pointed embroidery scissors is useful for trimming seams, snipping edges and for cutting yarns and threads. Finally, you will need a pair of sharp scissors for cutting card and paper. If you think you are likely to confuse your paper scissors with the fabric cutting pair, tie a piece of bright thread round the handle of one pair, so that you can quickly identify which is which.

Pinking shears are useful for cutting decorative edges on felt.

Cutting knives

You will need two kinds of craft knives: a heavy duty knife, like a Stanley knife or an X-acto knife, for cutting card, and a small knife, preferably a scalpel, for cutting thin card and paper. Use straight

blades as these suit most tasks and replace them often for the best results. Needless to say, these knives require care when in use. You should always cut straight lines by lining the knife up against a firm straight edge. Use a metal rule for this rather than a plastic or wooden ruler, as these materials can easily catch in the blade.

Pins and needles

When making toys of any kind, including puppets, it is a good idea to use as few pins as possible in case one gets lost inside the toy and becomes a source of danger later. Choose glass-headed

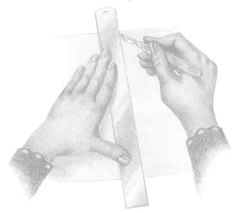

Line the knife up against a metal rule when cutting straight lines.

dressmaker's pins because these are easy to see on your work table (and on the floor) and there is less likelihood of their being misplaced. Count them as you use them in the fabric and again when they are removed to make sure that none are left in the puppet.

Quite a lot of the stitchery in puppet making is hand-sewing. The size of needle is often a personal preference, but medium-sized needles are best for general sewing while short, long-eyed crewel needles are used for embroidery.

A long darning needle is useful for working with knitting yarn (such as making puppets' hair). A bodkin is needed for threading elastic, ribbon or tape through casings.

Pencils and pens

Pencils are required for tracing or drawing patterns. A dressmaker's chalk pencil is invaluable for transferring marks from pattern to fabric. Felt-tipped pens in a variety of colours are used for marking symbols and letters on patterns and are also ideal for marking features on puppet heads.

Measuring aids

A tape measure is essential and you will also need a ruler to give a straight edge when drawing diagram patterns and cutting paper and card. You will see that measurements in this book are given first in imperial (inches) and then in metric (millimetres and centimetres). Use either imperial or metric measurements but do not combine the two because they may not work out exactly the same.

Stuffing tools

Sometimes, puppet heads and limbs are stuffed with toy filling and a special tool may be needed to push stuffing into place. Blunt pencils, knitting needles or even scissor points can be used, but if you are going to do a lot of puppet-making or toy-making, it is a good idea to make yourself a special stuffing tool. You need a short length of $\frac{1}{4}$in (6mm)-diameter wood dowelling – about 12in (30cm) will be sufficient. Shape one end to a blunt point, using first a craft knife and then sandpaper, until the point is smooth.

Other equipment

When you are handling paper and card, precise folding and creasing can be important. One very useful specialist tool for marking fold-lines on paper is a bookbinder's bone folder, which looks rather like a small modelling tool. This is drawn along against a straight edge and leaves a gentle groove ready for folding. You can improvise, however, by using a knitting needle or a blunt, curve-bladed table knife – or any other tool which creases rather than pierces the paper.

Score along lines before folding paper or thin card.

Adhesives

Choose the right adhesive for the job. PVA is a multi-purpose, easy-to-use adhesive, which can be used both as a glue and as a varnish (dilute it with water and brush over a surface for a glossy finish). Clear, quick-drying and non-trailing clear glue is also a good multi-purpose adhesive for card and paper. Use a glue spreader for an even coverage, or use the long tip for applying dots of adhesive. Stick adhesive is required for some projects. This type of adhesive comes in a twist-up tube and is easy to control. Advantages are that this glue does not dampen paper – and it is safe for children to use. Latex adhesive (white and dries clear) is ideal for sticking fabric to fabric or fabric to paper.

Adhesive tapes

In most crafts that involve paper, card and fabrics, you will need adhesive tape. Semi-transparent sticky tape is useful for holding paper and fabric edges together. You can also use tape to fix polythene and paper bags into shapes when constructing puppet heads.

Crumpled bags can be taped into shape to make puppet heads.

FABRICS AND MATERIALS

Generally, the pattern instructions for puppets recommend small amounts of plain or patterned fabrics, without colours or design being specified. Part of the fun in toy-making and puppet-making comes from using up bits of fabric left over from sewing projects. Often, quite small pieces are needed for a puppet's clothes and it is worth saving every scrap that comes your way. Ask dressmaking friends for left-over pieces and start a ragbag of oddments. Sometimes, bazaars or jumble sales have outgrown children's clothes for sale. Look these over carefully and see if less worn parts can be cut away and re-used. Wash fabrics thoroughly, discard the worn bits and iron the remaining scraps smooth.

When choosing colours for toys or puppets' clothes, colour, texture and pattern can be very important. Lightweight fabrics in clear tones or bright primaries, in plains or small-scale prints, should be your first choice. Avoid heavily embroidered fabrics and brocades unless your character puppet demands an ornate costume.

Interfacings

Non-woven interfacings are very useful in toy-making and in puppet-making. They can be used for backing thin fabrics and felt, and a backing of interfacing can help to control the stretch of knitted fabrics, which is a help when stuffing heads and arms. Lightweight interfacing is also ideal for making simple puppets' clothes. You can paint designs on to it and interfacing is non-fray, requiring minimal sewing.

FINISHING TOUCHES

Trimmings all help to finish a puppet's appearance and create the character. There are good ranges of trims in department stores and specialist craft shops and it is worth visiting these around sale times. Often, very small pieces of trims are on sale for next to nothing – useless for dressmaking but invaluable to a puppet-maker. Look for short ends of ribbons. They are available from a tiny $\frac{1}{16}$in (1.5mm) wide up to 3in (7.5cm) wide and the colour range is extensive. Cut-edge ribbons (acetate ribbons intended for gift-ties) are ideal for puppets. These are not washable or colour-fast but they come in patterns which you will find useful – tartans, checks, spots, jacquards, stripes etc. Narrow lace edgings and eyelet insertion can often be found and braids, plain and multi-coloured, in glittering lurex and silky finishes are worth searching for. Artificial flowers should be in your collection of puppet-making trimmings. Buy very cheap sprays and break them down into individual flowers.

Start a collection of tiny buttons, beads and sequins – and store away tinsel ribbons from Christmas parcels.

STUFFINGS

Some puppets may require heads or limbs to be stuffed. Polyester fibre toy filling is inexpensive and easy to use but there are other materials which will work just as well for puppets. Cotton wool and kapok make good, soft stuffings but for a next-to-no-cost filling, simply cut up old, discarded nylon tights and stockings.

PAPER AND CARD

Paper is used quite a lot in puppet-making. Some kinds of puppets are made entirely of construction paper. Gift-wrap paper is used to make or decorate character puppets' garments. Tissue paper, which comes in a wide range of colours, is useful for making accessories and for trimming. You can also utilize pieces of coloured paper from glossy magazines – snippets cut into shapes can look very decorative and jewel-like. Waste newsprint is used for papier mâché, for constructing puppet heads and hands.

Cardboard

Thin and medium-weight cardboard is often referred to in puppet-making instructions. Thin cardboard can be gleaned from cereal boxes or similar cartons – the weight is ideal. Heavier card is readily available in the cardboard outers discarded by supermarkets and other shops.

PATTERN-MAKING

The patterns in this book are given in three forms: direct trace-offs, diagrams with measurements indicated on them and graph patterns from which the pattern pieces can be enlarged.

Diagram patterns

It is recommended that these patterns are copied on to squared graph paper, using a ruler and sharply-pointed pencil. The lines on the paper will help you to keep corners square and accurate. If there are curves in the pattern, you will find that a flexible plastic ruler (obtainable from art suppliers) is a useful aid when drawing them. The ruler is bent into a curve and then you simply pencil along its edge. Once the pattern is drawn, the shapes can either be cut from the pattern paper or, if you want to keep the pattern for another time, traced on to tracing paper.

Direct trace-off patterns

To use these, you will need sheets of tracing paper or kitchen greaseproof

Direct tracing from the page.

paper. The paper is laid over the book page and taped down at the edges with small pieces of adhesive tape. Trace the image with a sharply pointed pencil.

Very simple shapes, such as eyes, noses or hands, may be drawn directly on to the wrong side of smooth fabric, using either a soft pencil or a dressmaker's chalk pencil. If fabrics are thin and transparent, patterns may be traced directly from the page.

> ### Working with felt
>
> Cut out shapes from felt in the same way as from woven fabric, pinning the paper pattern to it. When cutting out small shapes, either iron the felt on to interfacing to stiffen the edges or press the felt on to a small, self-adhesive label, removing afterwards.

Graph patterns

These patterns are given reduced in size on a squared grid. A scale is given and, to produce a full-sized pattern, you need squared dressmaker's paper marked with squares of the same scale. This paper is sold in large sheets, several to a packet, and can be obtained from dressmaking notions counters in department stores.

To reproduce a graph pattern, you copy the lines on your pattern paper, square for square. Incidentally, if squared paper is not easily available, you can mark large sheets of newspaper into squares of the right scale, using a felt-tipped pen and a ruler, and copy the pattern on to this.

Knitting needle sizes

Metric	(old sizes)	American
3.25mm	10	3
3.75mm	9	4
4mm	8	5
4.5mm	7	6
5mm	6	7
5.5mm	5	8
6mm	4	9
6.5mm	3	10

Knitting abbreviations

European		American	
k	knit	k	knit
p	purl	p	purl
st(s)	stitch(es)	st(s)	stitch(es)
dec	decrease	dec	decrease
inc	increase	inc	increase
tog	together	tog	together
rep	repeat	rep	repeat
rem	remaining	rem	remaining
cont	continue	cont	continue
foll	following	foll	following
st st	stocking stitch	st st	stockinette stitch
cast	off	bind	off

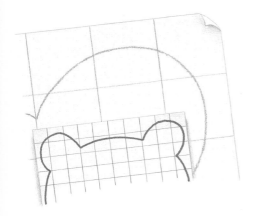

Enlarging a graph pattern.

KNITTED PUPPETS

Knitted puppets are great fun to make and only very simple stitches and techniques are involved. Almost any kind of wool yarn can be used for a puppet – chunky, double knitting, fancy yarns, bouclés etc – and often quite small amounts are needed. Most knitters have odd balls left over after knitting projects and these will be useful for your puppet-making stock. Alternatively, discarded knitted garments can be utilized. Unpick the seams and wash the separate pieces by hand in lukewarm suds. Rinse carefully, dry and then unravel the knitting, winding it into balls. If the wool has kinks in it and you prefer to reknit with smooth yarn, wind and tie the wool into hanks. Suspend the hank and hold a steaming kettle under it, gently pulling the end of the hank until the kinks straighten out. Leave to dry, then wind into balls.

STITCHING AND SEWING

In the instructions, stitching means working on a sewing machine and sewing means working by hand. However, if you want to work your puppet or its clothes entirely by hand, use small running stitches or neat back stitches.

SEWING STITCHES

For puppet-making, you will probably use only a few sewing stitches – basting, running stitch, back stitch and slip stitch. Oversewing, hemming stitch and ladder stitch are also useful for some projects.

Running stitch

This easy stitch is mostly used for joining two pieces of fabric together. It is also used for gathering up fabric. Begin with a small back stitch to secure the thread, pick up several small stitches on the needle and pull the needle through. Finish with a back stitch.

Gathering

Start with a back stitch, work running stitches along the gathering line and leave a length of thread at the end of the row for pulling up the gathers.

Slip stitch

This stitch is usually used for closing a seam. Work from right to left and bring the needle up through the folded edge of the fabric. Pick up a thread or two from the opposite fabric edge, then slip the needle through the folded edge for about $\frac{1}{8}$in (3mm). Bring the needle through and pull gently.

Basting

This is used to hold two pieces of fabric together temporarily. Work it in the same way as running stitch but make the stitches longer, about $\frac{1}{4}$in (6mm) long with $\frac{1}{4}$in (6mm) between each stitch.

Hemming

Hemming is worked from right to left, taking up 2 threads of the fabric at the fold of the hem. Insert the needle obliquely on the edge of the fold.

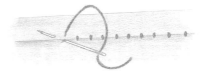

Oversewing

This is a useful stitch for joining the edges of felt pieces. Working from left to right, bring the needle through at A and insert the needle from the back of the work at B, bringing it through to the front at C, ready to start the next stitch. Keep stitches small and evenly spaced.

Ladder stitch

This stitch is used a great deal in toy-making and will be useful if you are attaching fabric ears, limbs etc. It is a simple running stitch, the stitches being taken first on one side of an opening, then on the other. As you work, turn the seam allowances to the inside with the needle point.

FANCY TRIMS
Pompons

Pompons are very easy to make and children will have great fun making them for their own puppets. Pompons are used for decoration of clothes, for noses, and for eyes. You can also make an entire puppet from pompons of different sizes.

Decide the size of the pompon and cut 2 circles of card. Cut holes from the centre to make card rings. Knot the end of the wool round the 2 rings, holding them together. Thread the other end of the wool into a large darning needle. Wind wool over the rings until the hole in the middle is filled. Using a sharp, pointed pair of scissors, snip into the layers of wool all round the edges of the rings. Take a short length of wool and slip it between the card rings. Tie the ends. Tear the card rings away from the wool pompon. Roll it in your hands to make the pompon round. Trim all over to even up the surface.

Knot the yarn end round two rings.

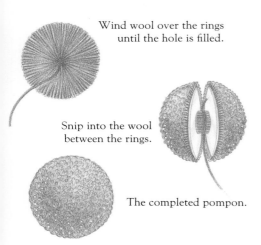

Wind wool over the rings until the hole is filled.

Snip into the wool between the rings.

The completed pompon.

Quick pompons

These are not as perfectly shaped as the pompons made on the card rings but they are adequate for decorating costumes. Wind wool round a narrow strip of card. Thread wool under the loops on one edge, slip the loops off the card and tie the ends of the wool. Cut the loops on the opposite edge to make the pompon. Trim to shape.

Bows

Although ribbon bows can be tied and then sewn in place, you will find the following method makes a better bow. Cut a piece of ribbon and form into a ring, the ends overlapping. Gather the middle, sewing through all thicknesses. Cut a small piece of ribbon, fold around the middle of the bow tightly and sew to secure it at the back. To give the bow tails, cut a piece of ribbon and fishtail the ends. Gather the middle and sew behind the bow.

Ruffles

Ruffles help to hide the join between puppet heads and bodies. You can use ribbon, fabric or even crêpe paper. Fold a strip lengthways, gather the doubled raw edge and sew the ruffle around the puppet's neck.

Tassels

Cut a length of wool, stranded embroidery thread or very narrow ribbon. Fold and refold the length until the bunch is about 3in (7.5cm) long. Tie a knot in the middle. Bring the side loops down and then bind round the bunch, just under the knot. Tie the knot ends tightly. Snip the folded ends.

Make tassels from wool, thread or narrow ribbon.

EMBROIDERY THREADS AND OTHER YARNS

Very little embroidery is involved in puppet-making, but you may sometimes want to embroider a face to get a special expression, or decorate a puppet's body or clothes. As puppets are not intended to be washed, almost any kind of thread or yarn can be used, such as fine twine, raffia, narrow gift-tie etc. Scraps of knitting yarn or embroidery wool work very well and look bright and colourful. Stranded embroidery cotton (use all six strands together for a bold effect) and pearl cotton both come in a wide range of shades. Soft embroidery cotton, a thick thread with a matt appearance, also looks pretty. Metallic threads are available in different colours and will add a touch of glitter to a puppet based on a fantasy figure such as a wizard or a fairy. These threads are also effective for scaly animals or birds' feathers.

Some eye effects using embroidery stitches together with circles of felt are shown on the right.

Collector's corner

One advantage of puppet-making is that you can use and recycle waste or throw-away material. Here are some of the things you can start collecting for your puppet-making sessions:
Plastic bottles
Egg-boxes
Cardboard or waxed paper cartons
Cardboard boxes in different sizes
Cartons (as a source of cardboard)
Corrugated card
Shredded plastic packing
Lengths of string and twine
Odd balls of knitting yarn
Scraps of coloured and plain fabrics
Scraps of felt
Coloured paper
Paper bags
Beads, buttons
Tinsel trims, braids, ribbons

EYES IDEAS

1 Circle of satin stitches

2 Straight stitches over a felt circle

3 Felt circle outlined in chain stitch

4 Pie slice cut from felt circle

5 Felt circle with straight stitches

6 Button sewn on, straight stitches

7 Straight stitches in a cross

EMBROIDERY STITCHES

Here are just a few stitches to help you to embroider puppets' faces.

Satin stitch

Work stitches evenly and so that they touch. Bring the needle through at A, insert it at B and bring it through again at C.

Straight stitch

Bring the needle through at A, insert it at B and bring it through again at C to form a star shape.

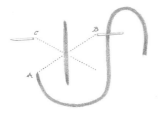

Back stitch

Bring the needle through at A, insert it at B and bring it out at C, in front of A.

Stem stitch

Bring the needle through at A, the thread below the needle. Insert it at B and bring it through again at C.

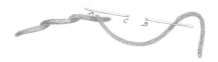

Chain stitch

Bring the needle through at A and, with the thread below the needle, insert it beside A at B. The thread forms a loop. Bring the needle through at C, pull through gently ready to start the next chain stitch. To secure at C, work a tying stitch over the loop.

French knot

Bring the needle through at A, wind the thread round the needle twice and then insert the point at B, close by A. Pull the thread through so that the knot tightens on the surface.

PAPIER MACHE

This is a fascinating craft and one that both children and adults can enjoy together. Practically no equipment – other than kitchen utensils – is needed and flour-and-water paste is very easily made.

In puppet-making, papier mâché is used to make puppets' heads and, sometimes, hands. There are several techniques in papier mâché but two specifically are used in puppet-making – layering and paper pulp modelling.

Layering method

In this, pasted strips of paper are applied to a mould, left to dry and then, afterwards, the shell is lifted off. All kinds of things can be used for moulds, depending on the shape you are creating. Inflated balloons make round or oval shapes and bowls make half-spheres. If you prefer, you can layer over a carton and leave the mould in place to strengthen the structure.

Basic technique

Grease the mould all over with petroleum jelly. Tear newspaper into small strips about ½in (1cm) wide and 2in (5cm) long. Dampen the strips in water and apply to the mould, overlapping the strips. Smooth each strip in place.

For the second and subsequent layers, put some mixed wallpaper paste into a shallow bowl and dip the paper strips into it. Apply all over the mould. Leave to dry thoroughly, then apply a third layer of pasted strips, this time working in the other direction (if the first and second layers were vertical, make this layer horizontal – it helps to strengthen the structure).

Add another layer of strips, working in the other direction again and continue until the layers are thick enough to hold the shape. You may need 6–10 layers.

Drying

Papier mâché will take several days to dry completely, so be patient if you want successful results. Keep the mould

If you are applying several layers of pasted paper to a mould, it helps to use paper of different types for each layer so that you can see that you have completely covered the surface.

propped up and leave to dry naturally in a warm, dry place.

Fine finish

Puppet heads will require a smooth finish before painting. When the last layer of newspaper strips has dried, tear white tissue paper into small pieces and paste all over the surface. Leave to dry, then apply a second layer. Remove the papier mâché from the mould by easing it off with a knife blade.

Smear petroleum jelly over the mould.

Tear newspaper into narrow strips.

106

Making your own paste

You may not want to let children work with wallpaper paste as some kinds have fungicides in them. Here is a simple method for making your own papier mâché paste.

Mix 8 tablespoons of plain white flour with 1 tablespoon of kitchen salt. Mix to a creamy consistency with cold water. Pour on boiling water, stirring all the while. The paste will turn translucent and thicken. Leave to cool. The paste will keep, covered, in a refrigerator, for 3–4 days.

Painting

Paint the papier mâché with white emulsion paint, then decorate with acrylic paints. Finish by painting with a coat of diluted PVA adhesive. If you prefer, you can use poster paints, varnishing afterwards, or modeller's gloss paints which are reasonably quick-drying.

Pulp papier mâché

This technique is more like modelling and is used to build up structures over a mould or for building up certain areas, like features on a puppet head. Grease the working surface with petroleum jelly and spoon on the pulp. Press it down firmly. Spoon on some more and begin modelling. Use modelling tools if possible, although pieces of cutlery such as a spoon handle or a knife tip will do almost as well, or simply use your fingers. Leave each layer to dry out completely before applying the next. If you are making puppets' hands or feet, cut the shape from cardboard first, apply 1–2 layers of pasted tissue paper, then build up the thickness with pulp.

A drying period of several days should be allowed for pulp work. Avoid using any means of speeding up the drying process as this may cause the pulp to crack or distort. If small cracks do appear while you are working, fill these with more pulp, smoothing off the surface.

Paper pulp

Dried powdered paper can be obtained which, when mixed with water and paste, makes very good paper pulp. However, here is a recipe for making your own pulp.

Materials

6 double sheets of newspaper
$\frac{1}{4}$ cup of fabric conditioner
7 large spoons of whiting or ground chalk
6 large spoons of wallpaper paste
2 medium-sized spoons of linseed oil
4 medium-sized spoons of PVA adhesive

Preparation

Tear the newspaper into small pieces. Put the paper into a large bucket and cover with water. Add the fabric conditioner. Leave the paper to soak for 12 hours.

Method

Pour the water and paper into a large pan and bring to a boil over heat. Simmer for 30 minutes. The paper will begin to break up. If a dark scum rises to the surface, skim this off. Leave the mixture to cool. Working in batches, mix, using a blender. Strain the pulp into a sieve and press with the back of a spoon to remove as much water as possible. Transfer the strained pulp to a large mixing bowl. Stirring well, mix in the whiting and wallpaper paste, then the linseed oil and PVA adhesive. Mix together thoroughly and the pulp is ready for use.

Paper pulp dries with quite a rough surface. You may want to finish off with 2–3 layers of pasted tissue paper and then a final coat of white emulsion paint before painting features etc.

Hairstyles

You can have a lot of fun with puppets' hairstyles, especially when you are creating fantasy characters. Thick knitting wool is effective and easy to work with, and makes good bunches and plaits. Raffia makes hair and beards for country characters. Strips cut from fabrics and stitched all over the head produce colourful effects – cut ½in (1cm)-wide strips with pinking shears and sew them all over the puppet head. Teased-out nylon twine makes wonderfully bushy hair – ideal for female puppets. Ordinary cotton wool or batting, too, make a quick and inexpensive hairstyle.

Hair with a centre parting stitched over a fringe.

Tied in bunches at the sides.

Try plaiting the side strands.

Puff puppet

This puppet is made from patchwork puffs. If you prefer an easier project, use circles of felt. Cut eight 6in (15cm) circles from different fabrics. Cut twenty-six 4in (10cm) circles of fabric. Work running stitches round all the circles. Pull up the gathers, tie off the ends. Flatten each puff. Cut 2 circles of white fabric 6in (15cm) in diameter and sew together right sides facing, leaving a 1in (2.5cm) gap. Turn right sides out, stuff for a head and embroider a clown's face. Sew on fabric strips for hair or work knitting wool loops. Thread the puffs on to elastic as shown. Cut hands and feet from felt and sew on. Fasten puppet strings to the back of the head, to each hand and to the two feet. Make a simple control bar. An animal puppet can be made in the same way.

Putting on a play

Puppets are great fun to make for their own sakes but, of course, the idea is that they are used to tell a story, and that means putting on a play.

The story

You can have a written script which all the puppeteers learn, or you can simply have an idea in your head of what the puppets will say, and then improvise. You may feel inspired to write your own story, but if you prefer, you can use a traditional tale, or even a play written for human or puppet actors. Alternatively, you could have no words at all, just using actions and perhaps music.

There are literally hundreds of stories to choose from, including stories from history and folklore worldwide, seasonal and religious stories, famous stories from literature or perhaps the story of a favourite famous person.

When choosing your characters, remember that you can mix and match sizes and methods of making puppets within a play. Perhaps you could have a knitted dragon, a string ghost and finger puppet fairies all on the same scene. It all depends on the requirements of your story and the number of puppeteers you have available to help you.

Music

Music is another wonderful way to tell a story. You could make your own, however simply, using drums, cymbals, comb and paper, and triangles, as well as singing and playing musical instruments. Or you could use records or tapes. Place someone in charge of music and let it take an important part in the script. It is a good idea to play music as an overture before the play begins. As the audience comes in, it makes them welcome, as well as setting the scene.

Sound effects

You could consider recording some of the more complicated sounds you might need, such as cars and trains, but there are other ways of making noises which require little or no equipment. Some people have an amazing talent for making sound effects with their own voices, so see if you can achieve a few of these noises: a squeaky door, water going down the plug-hole and dripping into the sink, eating noises, funny cartoon voices, and bird and animal noises.

Other impressive sound effects can be made with very simple equipment. For example, shake a large sheet of stiff card for thunder or roll pebbles or marbles in a cardboard box for storm noises. Drop a box of broken pieces of crockery for the sound of something breaking or pour water for the sound of running water. Use coconut shells for horses' hooves – it really does work.

Make a slap-stick for hitting noises which sound much worse than they are. To do this, find two flat thin sticks of the same length, perhaps slats from a fruit box. Bind them together at one end with string or adhesive tape and hit the floor, or something that will not be harmed, to make a slapping noise. This is how Punch and Judy take such a beating every day without disintegrating. Smooth the wood with sandpaper before use to avoid splinters.

The stage

The simplest stage of all is a large cardboard box with the base and most of the top cut away. It is placed on its side on a table, and the puppeteer works at one side while the audience views from the other. This is a perfectly satisfactory way of putting on a small show, but it is preferable to adapt whatever furniture you have available, as this gives a much bigger stage with more scope for the puppeteer, and therefore more for the audience to see.

Puppets can be operated very simply over the top of a sofa or through a kitchen hatch with a table in front of it. The best method, though, is to place a table in front of your audience and

A table and a concealed doorway form a versatile puppet theatre.

The curtain and pole are suspended from the door frame to hide the puppeteer.

The covered table provides a roomy stage for an action-packed play.

improvise a curtain which will hang down behind to leave a gap between it and the back of the table. This is where your puppets appear, while you are hidden by the curtain. This curtain can be hung across a doorway, across the corner of the room or from one high piece of furniture to another. Conceal offstage puppets, as well as yourself, behind the curtain, but do keep the puppets tidy and in the order in which they appear, so that the action is not delayed while you rummage around looking for the appropriate one. If you do a lot of plays, and if the table is old enough, you could put a row of hooks under the table edge and hang your puppets from them by loops in their skirts, like professional puppeteers do.

Presenting the characters
When you are operating your puppets in a play, you can emphasize their characters by the way you move them. String puppets can walk, skip or jump in a sprightly fashion or plod along slowly. Glove puppets can make expansive gestures with their arms and can clap, point or hide their faces. They are also adept at picking up props and even throwing them, with practice. Animals and fantasy figures can appear fierce, timid, graceful or bouncy. If you practise in front of a mirror, you will see your puppets as your audience will see them.

Acknowledgement

All the designs in this book are by the
author except *Jungle friend* on pages 46–49
which is the work of Cheryl Owen.

Other books in the Easy to Make series include:

Easy to Make: Dolls
by Audrey Vincente Dean

Easy to Make: Papier Mâché
by Lindy Tristram

Easy to Make: Flower Arranging
by Mary Lawrence

Easy to Make: Sewing
by Wendy Gardiner

Easy to Make: Christmas Crafts
by Kerrie Dudley

For more details of these books and
others in the series, please write to:
Anaya Publishers Ltd
Strode House
44–50 Osnaburgh Street
London NW1 3ND